Left Behind Or Sincerely Taken

Exposing the Myths of the Secret Rapture

By
Louis R. Torres

Printed by
Remnant Publications, Inc.

Left Behind or Sincerely Taken

This edition published 2001

Printed in the United States of America

ISBN 1-883012-91-0

Table of Contents

Throughout this publication all emphasis is supplied by the author unless otherwise noted and all Biblical references are from the King James Version unless otherwise indicated.

1

When the Clock Strikes Twelve

It's near midnight in Alexandria, Virginia, and most of the town is asleep. Except for a groggy attendant manning the all-night gas station or a few sleepy nurses making their hourly rounds. There is only one woman awake. She is trembling now, sitting bolt upright in her sweat-soaked bed, sorting the fears in her frazzled mind.

"Where am I? Who am I?" She grips her head in her hands. "Why am I here?"

The clock strikes twelve as her eyes adjust to the dark and familiar surroundings of her bedroom, and it's not until then that the welcome truth dawns. This nightmare—this horrible terror just past—has been only a dream.

Evangeline sighs and, sinking into her pillow, relives it once more:

She had been driving home from her job at Prudential when it happened. Just east of Tyson's Corner, on the Washington D.C. beltway, a Southwinds motor home swerved right across her lane! There hadn't been time to think. Jamming on the brakes of her '92 Camry, Evangeline skidded to a stop as the Southwinds bounced from one guardrail into another.

As a witness to the accident, Evangeline had waited in her car for the state police to arrive. When she finally did get out and walk up to the motor home, Evangeline was just in time to meet a puzzled patrolman stepping out of the door.

"Where is the driver?" he wanted to know. "There's no one here."

"That just can't be," Evangeline replied, "I've been here since the accident, and no one left!"

Ms. Sincere didn't know it then, but most of the highways in the Washington, D.C., area were already blocked by similar accidents. News commentators reported still-fastened seatbelts, shaken passengers insisted that drivers had "just disappeared," while equally shaken drivers described one or more "vanishing" passengers.

At this point, Evangeline's dream had shifted to the CNN evening news. There she had learned that thousands of "driverless" happenings had taken place all over the world. Pilotless planes crash-landed with or without their passengers, trains hurtled down the tracks minus their engineers, and an ominous number of ocean liners had reported missing seaman, whom they could only assume had fallen overboard.

Could the secret rapture have happened without her? Frantically, Evangeline tried calling her parents, but they "weren't home." She dialed her best friends, but they too were "missing." In her heart, she knew what had happened. Operation "Evacuation Earth" had begun—and she had been "left behind!"

"Left behind" to suffer the seven years of tribulation! "Left behind" to endure the reign of the Antichrist in Jerusalem! "Left behind" to hear the seven blasts of God's trumpet announcing the seven great plagues!

"I've been left! I've been left! I've been left!" Evangeline wrung her hands and sobbed in despair—which is how she finally found herself, drenched with sweat, fumbling for a phone in the darkness, yet safe in the middle of her own queen-sized bed.

Reaching for a light, Evangeline pulls out her Bible and starts to read:

> "I tell you, in that night there shall be two men in one bed; the one shall be taken, and the other shall be left. Two women shall be grinding together; the one shall be taken, and the other left. Two men shall be in the field; the one shall be taken, and the other left" (Luke 17:34–36).

> "Then shall two be in the field; the one shall be taken, and the other left. Two women shall be grinding at the mill; the one shall be taken, and the other left" (Matthew 24:40–41).

Evangeline sinks back into her pillow, closing her eyes in relief. She is so happy this was only a dream, though she knows it won't always be so. With many in the Christian world, Evangeline believes that there will be a secret rapture—that one day soon, the righteous will simply disappear, being secretly "taken" from this planet. She believes that the wicked will most certainly be left behind to suffer the "great tribulation," and that Antichrist will reign for a time in Jerusalem until the end of the seven years. Then, she believes, Jesus Christ will come to deliver His people.

Most recently, Evangeline's belief in the secret rapture has been stirred by the *Left Behind* series. These books, the best-selling Christian fiction of all time, tell the riveting stories of people who, after the rapture of the church, find themselves "left behind" to experience the great tribulation. With an imaginative interpretation of the Bible as the background, this apocalyptic fiction has captured the hearts of literally millions of readers.

Serious Consequences

Best-seller lists aside, it's important for Christians and non-Christians alike to realize that the teaching of the secret rapture is fraught with serious consequences. If there is a secret rapture, there is also a second chance for the "wicked." If there is a second chance, some people will be tempted to take it. To make the most of their opportunity and have their party here and now—knowing that though they may suffer—they will have seven years to "clean up their act" before Jesus finally comes.

This is dangerous theology. If the rapture teachings are wrong, millions or even billions of people may be counting on a "second chance" when in fact there is none.

How would it feel to find there is no recourse—no opportunity to reverse a series of sin-filled habits and live for God at last? How would it feel to face a dreaded and catastrophic end? While this is not a happy thought, it is one we must consider. There is much at stake, and we all have something to lose if the teachings about the secret rapture aren't true.

In light of the seriousness of this issue and the widespread belief that the secret rapture and/or Jesus is coming soon, it seems especially important to know just what the Bible does say about the Second Coming of Christ. If you were expecting a visit from some earthly dignitary, it seems likely that you would want to know:

- who is coming
- how he is coming
- where he is coming

- when to expect him, and
- why he is coming

If you don't know who is coming or how he is coming, you might be deceived by an imposter. If you don't know when or where he is coming, you might be in the right place at the wrong time, or even the wrong place at the right time. And if you don't know why he is coming, you might not bother to be ready.

Of course, if we would know all this for some earthly dignitary, how much more should we be prepared for the most climactic event to take place on this earth since the First Coming of Jesus Christ? For if you don't know who Jesus is or how He is coming, you might be deceived by the devil. If you don't know when or where He is coming, you might not be ready to meet Him. And if you don't know why He is coming, you might not understand why you should even get ready.

With these thoughts in mind, let us set all fiction aside. It is time to hear the truth—the beautiful truth of the Second Coming as taught so profoundly in God's Holy, Inspired Word. Would you like to know the "who, what, when, where and why" of Christ's Second Coming? Then please turn the page, for a fact-filled, Bible-based study designed to help you be ready for that great and soon-coming event.

2

Who is Coming?

"This Same Jesus"

It would be hard, if not impossible, to meet any person at the airport if you didn't know who you were looking for. Similarly, one of the most important facets of being ready for the return of our Lord is a knowledge of "who" is coming.

God understands this, which is why, right after Christ's ascension, He had an angel tell the disciples that "this *same Jesus*" would someday come again. The angel wanted to make it emphatically clear that it would be this *same* Jesus and not another. It would be the *same* exact Jesus who had walked, prayed, eaten, and communed with His disciples—the One who brought the dead back to life, gave sight to the blind, comforted their hearts, stilled the storm and calmed their fears. Yes, he assured them, it is the *same One* whom you saw crucified, who was laid in the tomb, and who rose again. The *same One* you saw in the upper room after the resurrection and with whom you have spent the most thrilling moments of your life. "This *same Jesus* . . . shall so come in like manner as ye have seen him go into heaven" (Acts 1:11).

Not A Resurrected Ghost

Many people today believe, as did the disciples initially, that Jesus rose from the grave as a spirit. But the Bible states plainly that this is not the case:

Shortly after the resurrection, the disciples had sequestered themselves in the upper room for fear of the Jews (see John 20:19). Just a few days prior, they had witnessed the fury of the Jewish leaders unleashed, turning all their hopes and dreams into dark forebodings and terrible apprehensions. Confused and terrified, they feared for their future. Suddenly Jesus stood in their midst, saying, "Peace be unto you. But they were terrified and affrighted, and supposed that they had seen a spirit" (Luke 24:36–37).

Their superstitions led them to the wrong conclusion. They supposed they were seeing a ghost, or spirit. They were obviously still confused about Jesus' teaching. To calm their fears, Jesus said to them, "Why are ye troubled? and why do thoughts arise in your hearts? Behold my hands and my feet, that it is I myself" (Luke 24:38–39). The Bible emphasizes the pronoun "I" with the additional, reflective pronoun "myself" to make plain that it was actually Jesus, not another. He left no room for doubt.

From this statement of self-identification, Jesus went on to concretely prove the veracity of His declaration. He said to them, "Handle me and see; for a spirit hath not flesh and bones as ye see me have" (Luke 24:39).

Jesus drove the point home that He had returned from the tomb with flesh and bones. (You can read the account for yourself in Luke 24.) The disciples were amazed! "And while they yet believed not for joy, and wondered, he said unto them, Have ye here any meat?" (Luke 24:41). It was not until after they saw Him eat that they were glad (see John 20:20).

Just think how they must have felt. They must have become ecstatic as the reality really struck home. One can only imagine them leaping for joy, with tears of exuberance flowing down their faces, exclaiming "It is Jesus!" Their Lord and Saviour had actually come back from the dead! It was "this same Jesus" who appeared to them in the upper room, and, forty days later, it was "this same Jesus" who ascended up into the skies before their very eyes.

His death and resurrection shed even more light on this truth. When Christ died on Calvary, He died as a man. He had "flesh and bones"—a physical body. And though many are not aware of it, it is a Biblical fact that Jesus also came forth in the resurrection in a human, bodily form.

Why is this point important? Because by living, dying, and rising again as a man, Jesus gave mankind the wonderful hope of the resurrection. Though we die, we, too, may live again through His glorious power (see John 11:25).

Jesus demonstrated His power over death not only at His resurrection, but also during His earthly ministry. Lazarus had been dead for four days, but was brought back to life in the flesh (see John 11:43–44). The widow's son (see Luke 7:12–15) and Jairus's daughter (see Luke 8:49–55) were also resurrected by Christ. Yet neither came back as spirits. Both returned to life physically and in bodily form. In the Old Testament the same reality is revealed. The son of the woman of Zarephath (see 1 Kings 17:17–23), the Shunammite's son (see 2 Kings 4:32–37), and the young man laid in Elisha's sepulchre (see 2 Kings 13:21), were all resurrected. They all rose to live normal lives. Job's belief in this hope of living again is eloquently recorded in the Old Testament: "I know that my redeemer liveth, and that he shall stand at the latter day upon the earth: and though after my skin worms destroy this body, yet in my flesh shall I see God: whom I shall see for myself, and mine eyes shall behold, and not another; though my reins be consumed within me" (Job 19:25–27).

Let us consider Adam, the father of the human race. If he had never sinned, he would have lived forever as a man in bodily form. You and I are descendants of Adam, and, as a result, we have the same nature. Because Adam partook of sin, he became subject to death. This death was then transmitted to his posterity. In the words of Paul, "Wherefore, as by one man sin entered into the world, and death by sin; and so death passed upon all men, for that all have sinned" (Romans 5:12).

Because of His great love for us, God gave us the promise of life through the resurrection. The promise of eternal life can only be realized in Jesus, who said, "I am the resurrection, and the life: he that believeth in me, though he were dead, yet shall he live!" (John 11:25). Man lost eternal life through sin, but through Jesus Christ he can gain it back. "For our conversation is in heaven; [the scripture declares] from whence also we look for the Saviour, the Lord Jesus Christ: who shall change our vile body, that it may be fashioned like unto his glorious body, according to the working whereby he is able even to subdue all things unto himself" (Philippians 3:20–21).

That is why Paul says, "Forasmuch then as the children are partakers of flesh and blood, he also himself likewise took part of the same; that through death he might destroy him that had the power of death, that is, the devil; and deliver them who through fear of death were all their lifetime subject to bondage" (Hebrews 2:14–15).

And it is this Jesus—this "flesh and bones" *very same* Jesus who lived and suffered and died for us, who has promised to come and take us home. We are waiting for Him—not a spirit or a "spiritual second coming," but a literal, physical return just as personal and real as the first advent. Now *that's* something to look forward to!

The "Genuine" Jesus

While I was lecturing in the city of Tirgu Mures, Romania, a woman requested an appointment with me. At the appointed time, she pulled a folded-up newspaper page out of her purse and pointed to an ad placed by an American company. The ad, which offered home-based employment, suggested that materials sent from the States could be assembled in the recipient's home. The end product, which was supposedly expensive, hand-crafted earrings, could then be shipped back to the company to be examined. Upon completion of the inspection, the company would either accept or reject the workmanship. Workers whose jewelry was approved could have it sold in the American market, netting them five to six hundred dollars a month. This was a salary large enough to make them the envy of Romanian military captains, who made only $40.00 per month.

There was one unalterable condition to be met, however, before the first kit could be received. Interested persons must send $75.00 to the company in the form of a certified bank note. Upon receipt of the correct amount and necessary forms, the promised materials would be mailed and the money-making venture would begin. In response to the ad, she sacrificed, raised the money and sent it off.

Looking at the supposed valuable beads to be assembled, (the total of which could be bought at a Woolworth store for about $1.50) and at the well-made earrings she had put together, I felt great pity for this hard-working but naïve lady. Feeling deeply for her great loss, and not knowing how to confirm her fears that perhaps "it was too good to be true," I reluctantly broke the news that she had indeed been taken in. With shattered hopes and tearful eyes, the poor woman turned and departed. I was able to empathize with her, for the memories were very fresh of a time when I, too, had been taken.

We are often amused when witnessing others being tricked by some prank. Sometimes we are amazed at how gullible "they" can be. Yet we cease to see the humor when these things happen to us. It is true that at times the loss is not enormous, and we laugh at ourselves, wondering, "How could we have fallen for that?" Yet there are times and circumstances when financial, or other losses, are devastating. Regardless of how great or small our material loss may be, there is something far more important, and even greater, to consider than our temporal misfortunes: the impact that being "taken" can have on our spiritual and eternal well-being.

A Similar Story

For hundreds of years severe political struggles had plagued the small country of Albania. Finally, freedom day came July 29, 1913, with the much desired and long-awaited independence. But a serious problem soon surfaced, for the courageous freedom fighters had neither a president nor a king. Strangely enough, the people asked Halim Eddine, a prince in the country from which they had just won independence, to come and lead their nation.

The Turkish Prince Eddine was not sure he wanted to be the king of Albania, so for some time he neglected to send a response. The people became anxious. Then one day a telegram arrived stating that the Prince was on his way to Durazzo, the capital city.

A few days later the new leader arrived in a golden coach. He wore a striking uniform decorated with medals. At his side he carried a shining sword. He was tall and carried himself with the stately bearing of a king. When he spoke, everyone listened. For five days, he was honored at banquets and parades throughout the city—that is until another telegram arrived from the Sultan of Turkey. Much to the surprise of the Albanians, the telegram stated that Prince Eddine was still in Turkey. In other words, the man in Durazzo was an imposter!

In disbelief, the people hurried to the "prince" for an explanation, but wisely, he had already vanished! As it turned out, his name was actually Otto Witte, a circus performer who closely resembled Prince Eddine.

How Could This Happen?

How could the Albanians have been fooled by a talented actor who turned out not to be the prince at all, but a traveling circus performer? Perhaps the answer lies in one of the basic laws of human nature. Have you ever noticed that when the stress is the greatest, so are the blunders? It is a fact that the higher the level of emotions or anxiety, the lower the level of calm, balanced judgment. The greater the need, the more serious the situation—the more weakened are our tools of defense and discrimination.

Consider the young husband who has just discovered that his dearly beloved wife is having an extra-marital affair. If his reactions are average, he will explode in a fit of emotion, face flushed, eyes flashing, and arms flailing threateningly. There he is, faced with the possibility of losing his most prized possession—his wife, his heart—and he says all the wrong things in all the wrong ways. Why?—Because his intense state of emotion has unbalanced his judgment.

What about the dear souls who discover they have cancer? Not a few start trying everything imaginable (and unimaginable) to discover and experience a cure. Add to this the long list of political agreements made during severe economic times, together with their unhappy results, and you have a sad history—simply the result of emotional misjudgment.

Yes, when we hurt, when we are suffering, when we are anxious or impatient, we become easy victims of misjudgment. But, even more disturbing, we become easy victims of deception and fraud. We are, at such times, wide open to impostors and the counterfeit, for our discernment is dead.

It is just such situations and circumstances that result in riots and/or crowd action. Emotions spread faster than judgment, actions faster than concepts, mob instinct faster than individual decision. When it is all over, much has happened, but few are really sure "what" or "why."

Does it Have to Be This Way?

As obvious as the human weakness of making emotional misjudgments is, it still seems to take us by surprise. Over and over, we find ourselves "victimized"—taken advantage of. It may be the common, everyday "victimization" by our children playing on our emotions, or the salesman, or the lover; or it may be the more serious victimization by government espionage, by civic fraud, or, saddest of all, by religious opportunists, false christs, "holy men," and unfamiliar "circuit" preachers.

We are living in stressful times. The future looks bleak and uncertain. Tension is high and many are looking for different escape routes! But we must not allow our anxiety to lead us to trust in false spiritual securities—or promises that are like ropes of sand.

As the Albanians were taken in by Otto Witte, the circus actor—so today many stand the chance of being taken—taken by deception, and finally by the swift destruction that will come to the unprepared.

Do not be the one taken in. Rather, be among the ones who, while remaining alive, shall be caught up at Christ's glorious appearing and receive eternal life. Then the promise made (see Revelation 21:3–5) will be realized—and you will never be taken in again.

There is very clear-cut evidence in the Scriptures that Jesus has guarded the way He will return. He has declared that when He comes, every eye will see Him. All the angels will come with Him. If the glory of one angel was able to knock down a hundred Roman soldiers stationed at Christ's tomb, can you imagine what the glory of ten thousand times ten thousand, and thousands of thousands of angels will be like?

A few months after my decision to become a Christian, I had a dream. I was in New York City, sitting in my mother's apartment. Suddenly a great brightness coming in through the window gripped my attention. As I looked out the window, I saw the whole heavens lighted up more brilliantly than I had ever seen them before. My heart raced! I kept looking up; my eyes fixed on the scene. I saw the atmosphere filled with myriads of celestial beings, and it was awesome! As I continued gazing at the splendor, there appeared one sitting on a throne, encircled with glory. My heart leaped as I realized—and I remember saying it aloud—"Jesus is coming!" I quickly ran outside and began to look for my family to tell them that Jesus was coming. Then I awoke. What a dream! I do not remember having such thrilling joy at any other time as I had in experiencing that dream.

Yes, then it was only a dream, but soon it will be a reality. What a wonderful day it will be when He comes! Many of God's people in the past have died with the hope of seeing Jesus come. John's final prayer was, "Even so, come, Lord Jesus" (Revelation 22:20). He had a real hope in a real God who could save real people. And as with those in times past, you, too, can have this glorious hope in a soon-coming Redeemer.

Soon Jesus will come. He will appear literally and bring an end to sin and all of its tragic results. At last there will come the day when we will never be ***taken*** in again. There is a real God coming for real people. This thought should inspire a resounding note of praise. With John the revelator, we should be moved to exclaim, "Amen. Even so, come, Lord Jesus."

3

Why is He Coming?

To Marry His Bride, the Church

Jesus is coming again! The Bible leaves no room for question concerning this fact—and it also tells us why He is coming again.

In fact, several scriptural reasons are given for the second advent.

Reason #1: He Has Promised

The first reason for the Second Coming is, of course, that Jesus has promised to come again. "Let not your heart be troubled: ye believe in God, believe also in me. In my Father's house are many mansions: if it were not so, I would have told you. I go to prepare a place for you. And if I go and prepare a place for you, I will come again, and receive you unto myself; that where I am, there ye may be also" (John 14:1–3).

Jesus tells us that He "is not slack concerning his promise, as some men count slackness" (2 Peter 3:9), and, since not one of His promises which He made has failed, we can trust in His word.

Reason #2: He Will Redeem His Investment

Jesus has made an investment in each of us which He considers so precious that He must come to retrieve it." In the words of the apostle Paul: "Ye are bought with a price" (1 Corinthians 6:20).

Peter exclaims, "Forasmuch as ye know that ye were not redeemed with corruptible things, as silver and gold, from your vain conversation received by tradition from your fathers; but with the precious blood of Christ, as of a lamb without blemish and without spot" (1 Peter 1:18–19).

Though silver and gold were at His disposal, yet, He thought our worth of so great value that He paid the price of redemption with His own blood. He will also come to reclaim the earth: to be re-established as the rightful Ruler of the world, and to destroy sin, its originator, and its propagators forever.

Reason #3: He ComesFor His Bride—All of the Saved!

A Scriptural analogy used to illustrate another reason for the return of Jesus is found in 2 Corinthians 11:2: "For I am jealous over you with godly jealousy: for I have espoused you to one husband, that I may present you as a chaste virgin to Christ."

The dictionary definition for the word "espoused" is "to promise to marry." Today we call it being "engaged" to be married. However, unlike the light manner in which some take this commitment in our day, the oriental betrothal was a binding contract that was entered into with solemn promises and the payment of money. In addition, it could be broken only by a divorce.

In ancient times, a middleman was employed to make arrangements for the betrothal of a son or daughter (see Matthew 25:1–13; 1 Corinthians 7:36–38). For practical purposes, an ancient betrothal was as binding as the marriage itself. The bride-elect either remained at home with her parents or was committed to the care and protection of trusted friends of the bridegroom until the husband-elect should come for her. Often considerable time elapsed between the betrothal and the wedding, but during this time, all communication between the future husband and the bride-to-be was carried on through a trusted friend.

John the Baptist understood that he was playing the role of the friend of the bridegroom. He made this plain when he responded to those seeking to stir up jealousy in him toward Christ by saying, "He that hath the bride is the bridegroom: but the friend of the bridegroom, which standeth and heareth him, rejoiceth greatly because of the bridegroom's voice: this my joy therefore is fulfilled" (John 3:29).

The ancient practice of betrothal was reinforced in Mary's and Joseph's experience. "Now the birth of Jesus Christ was on this wise: When as his mother Mary [the mother of Jesus] was espoused to Joseph, before they came together, she was found with child of the Holy Ghost. Then Joseph her husband, being a just man, and not willing to make her a publick example, was minded to put her away privily. But while he thought on these things, behold, the angel of the Lord appeared unto him in a dream, saying, Joseph, thou son of David, fear not to take unto thee Mary thy wife: for that which is conceived in her is of the Holy Ghost" (Matthew 1:18–20).

Though Joseph was only betrothed, the angel calls Mary his wife. Upon discovering that she was pregnant, he decided to put her away, or divorce her. But the angel intervened, and "then Joseph being raised from sleep did as the angel of the Lord had bidden him, and took unto him his wife" (Matthew 1:24).

This analogy of the ancient engagement reveals some precious lessons.

- Jesus left heaven—His home. The scripture says, "For this cause shall a man leave his father and mother, and shall be joined unto his wife, and they two shall be one flesh" (Ephesians 5:31).
- He came to this earth to become engaged to His bride, the church He is committed! He has bound Himself with a solemn oath.
- He went to heaven to prepare for the wedding, while His bride, the church (which means among other things, all of God's believers), was left to prepare herself for her husband-to-be.

Eventually the time will come when Heaven will pronounce, "Let us be glad and rejoice, and give honour to him: for the marriage of the Lamb is come, and his wife hath made herself ready. And to her was granted that she should be arrayed in fine linen, clean and white: for the fine linen is the righteousness of saints" (Revelation 19:7–8). Much time has elapsed from the time Jesus espoused Himself to His church. He longs for the day that He can come to get His bride.

Jesus went to His Father's house to make the preparations. "In my Father's house are many mansions: if it were not so, I would have told you. I go to prepare a place for you. And if I go and prepare a place for you, I will come again, and receive you unto myself; that where I am, there ye may be also" (John 14:2–3).

This is betrothal language. Jesus is in heaven getting things ready for the marriage, and He has promised, "I will come again." But the bride must make herself ready in order for Him to come. She does this by availing herself of, and putting into practice, all that Heaven has provided for that preparation. When she (or we) are ready, Heaven will mark the fact, and Jesus, the bridegroom, will descend to take His bride (the church) home (see Revelation 19:11–16).

Jesus said, "I will come again." The dictionary definition for "again" is: "once more; a second time; anew." (*Webster's New World Dictionary*, College edition, 1968, The World Publishing Company, Cleveland and New York.) With this definition and the concept of espousal in mind, it is clear that the word "again" indicates that He is returning, or coming once more for His bride. He came once and dwelt among us. He betrothed Himself to us, and then left with the vow of returning to take His bride.

If we compare this to the analogy that He gave us, we will agree that no marriage practice on earth has the bridegroom returning several times to take only a part of his wife-to-be. Praise God! Jesus is coming very soon, coming *once and for all* to take His *complete wife*!

Illustration by Lars Justinen

4

How is He Coming

"In Like Manner..."

In order to understand just how Jesus will return, let us take a look at the manner of His earthly departure. By understanding how He left, we may be able to arrive at the proper conclusion concerning the manner of His return. The New Testament book of Acts, chapter 1, sets the scene for us.

After His resurrection, Jesus had spent several days with His disciples. Finally, the unannounced moment of His departure had come. "When He had spoken these things, while they beheld, He was taken up, and a cloud received Him out of their sight. And while they looked steadfastly toward heaven as He went up, behold, two men stood by them in white apparel; which also said, Ye men of Galilee, why stand ye gazing up into heaven? This same Jesus which is taken up from you into heaven, shall so come in like manner as ye have seen him go into heaven" (Acts 1:9-11).

There they stood talking to the Lord on the mount. Suddenly and without any prior notice, He began to rise into the air before their very eyes. "He was taken up." And as He ascended, their sights were fixed on Him. Up, up, He went, disappearing out of sight just like a balloon. Wouldn't it have been marvelous to watch that event? Think of the excitement to have been able to witness a man rising into the air without the aid of any mechanical device! Then there was the angel by their siding, promising that their Lord would come again "in like manner."

Here, in these angelic words, we hear an authoritative declaration regarding the manner of Christ's return. Since Jesus was seen being lifted up and departing from planet Earth, then His return must emulate His physical and visible departure.

Now let us consider several questions regarding His departure and soon return:

The Way He Left

The answer to this question is found in Acts 1:9-11. The record says that a "cloud received Him out of their sight." In Psalms 104:3 the Bible says that the clouds are "chariots," and Psalms 68:17 identifies the chariots as the "angels" of God. So we can conclude that a cloud of angels escorted Him home. What a great procession that must have been as the angelic host ushered their beloved Lord home!

Where He Went

The angel answered this question, telling the disciples that He "is taken up from you into heaven." Heaven is the abode of the Father and of all the loyal angels.

That the Father is in heaven and that Jesus believed it is clear from the model prayer that He gave us. He taught us to pray, "Our Father which art in Heaven" (Matthew 6:9). This fact of God's heavenly abode is established throughout the Bible. In the Old Testament Moses wrote, "Look down from thy holy habitation, from heaven" (Deuteronomy 26:15). In the dedication of the earthly temple King Solomon prayed, "And hearken thou to the supplication of thy servant, and of thy people Israel, when they shall pray toward this place: and hear thou in heaven thy dwelling place: and when thou hearest, forgive" (1 Kings 8:30). In the New Testament, Stephen, the deacon, in his final address to the Jews just before his execution, said "Howbeit the most High dwelleth not in temples made with hands, as saith the prophet, Heaven is my throne, and earth is my footstool: what house will ye build me? saith the Lord: or what is the place of my rest?" (Acts 7:48-49)

Heaven is the place Jesus ascended to. Mark 16:19 says, "So then after the Lord had spoken unto them, he was received up into heaven, and sat on the right hand of God." And the apostle Luke wrote, "He was parted from them, and carried up into heaven" (Luke 24:51). Yes, our Lord went to heaven, and He will descend from the same place to gather His children home.

How He Went

The Bible tells us that Jesus left with clouds of angels, and He will return with clouds of angels. Notice Revelation 1:7: "Behold, he cometh with clouds; and every eye shall see him." As Jesus told His disciples, "When the Son of man shall come in his glory, and all the holy angels with him, then shall he sit upon the throne of his glory" (Matthew 25:31). Think of the splendor, the skies ablaze with Heaven's angelic host!

The Second Coming will be a global event for "every eye shall see Him." The Bible contradicts the declaration of many ministers today that "only the righteous will see and hear Him."

"Every eye means every eye that has spiritual discernment," is the popular teaching of the day. But the Bible says "and they also which pierced Him" will see Him. Then the verse concludes with these words, "and all the kindred of the earth shall wail because of Him."

Those who pierced Him certainly did not have spiritual discernment, neither do those who "wail because of Him." These above-mentioned statements are sometimes used to allude to some secret coming detected only by a select group. But the Scriptures declare that He will *appear.*

Note the following texts:

- "And then shall ***appear*** the sign of the Son of Man in heaven: and then shall all the tribes of the earth mourn, and they shall see the Son of man coming in the clouds of heaven with power and great glory" (Matthew 24:30)
- "That thou keep this commandment without spot, unrebukeable, until the ***appearing*** of our Lord Jesus Christ: which in his times he shall shew, who is the blessed and only Potentate, the King of kings, and Lord of lords (1 Timothy 6:14-15).
- "I charge thee therefore before God, and the Lord Jesus Christ, who shall judge the quick and the dead at His ***appearing*** and His kingdom (2 Timothy 4:1)
- "That the trial of your faith, being much more precious than of gold that perisheth, though it be tried with fire, might be found unto praise and honour and glory at the ***appearing*** of Jesus Christ" (1 Peter 1:7)
- "And when the chief Shepherd shall ***appear,*** ye shall receive a crown of glory that fadeth not away" (1 Peter 5:4)

These texts speak emphatically of the Second Coming as a literal, visible event when Christ will actually appear. In the *Strong's Concordance* the Greek words in the above-mentioned text are:

- *Epiphaneia,* which means a manifestation, appearing or brightness, and
- *Phaino,* which means to lighten, show, seem, be seen or shine.

These references can lead to no other conclusion than that the coming of the Lord will be conspicuous, distinguishable, clear to the sight, and obvious. Even the crown mentioned in 1 Peter 5:4 contradicts the idea of something invisible. For if the "crown fadeth not away," it must certainly be visible or seen.

That everyone will see Him, including the wicked, is certain. A vivid picture of this fact is dramatically revealed in Revelation 6, where the revelator describes the reaction of the wicked. "And the kings of the earth, and the great men, and the rich men, and the chief captains, and the mighty men, and every bondman, and every free man, hid themselves in the dens and rocks of the mountains; and said to the mountains and rocks, Fall on us, and hide us from the face of Him that sitteth on the throne, and from the wrath of the Lamb: for the great day of his wrath is come; and who shall be able to stand?" (Revelation 6:15-17)

The whole language here is not symbolic, but literal. The frightful pleas of the wicked to inanimate objects, together with their attempts to find refuge or flee, give evidence not of a surreal, but an actual happening.

What a terrible day it will be for those horror-stricken souls! They will finally resort to prayer on that day, but unfortunately, they will not be praying to God to save them, but to the rocks and mountains to fall on them and hide them from the face of Him who sitteth on the throne. Yes, every eye of every person who is alive, the righteous and the wicked, will see Him someday soon!

A Worldwide, Global Event

The Bible also tells us that Jesus' second coming will be global in nature. In other words, the entire world will be involved. Jesus declared, "And then shall appear the sign of the Son of man in heaven: and then shall all the tribes of the earth mourn" (Matthew 24:30). This language is all-inclusive. No one is exempt. "All the tribes of the earth mourn" because of Him. And why are they mourning? Because they are confronted with the reality—Jesus has come, and they are unprepared to receive Him in peace. Notice the next part: "and they shall see the Son of man coming in the clouds of heaven with power and great glory."

The question has been asked, How will it be possible for every eye to see Him when He appears? First of all, with God, nothing is impossible. How it will take place, no one really knows. Perhaps the following example can help us visualize one possibility.

Because of Australia's location, people on that continent can see the constellation called the Southern Cross. Those who live in the United States, on the other hand, cannot see it. Instead, Americans are able to see the North Star, which those "down under" are unable to view. However, there is one constellation that all can see, and that constellation is Orion. Orion moves from the east to the west. Just as Orion can be seen moving westward from all points of the inhabited globe, so should every eye on planet Earth be able to see Him as He approaches from the East (see Matthew 24:27).

Yes, we shall behold Him. For with authority Jesus reaffirmed, "Hereafter shall ye see the Son of man sitting on the right hand of power, and coming in the clouds of heaven" (Matthew 26:64). Reader, it may be that you and I will be among the millions who will be alive to witness the most stupendous event of Earth's history—the second coming of Christ.

5

When is He Coming

Very Soon, But We "Know Not the Hour"

One of the prerequisites to being ready for Jesus to come is knowing "when" to expect Him. And while the Bible makes it clear that "no man knows the day or the hour" (Matthew 24:36; Mark 13:32), it also admonishes Christians to live in a constant state of readiness. Unfortunately, the Second Coming, which should be the source of the Christian's greatest joy and hope, has also provided the impetus for some of the world's greatest delusions. In fact, history is littered with the false hopes, false starts, and unmet expectations of date-setting believers.

The Dangers of Date Setting

The Australian rapturists who expected our Lord's return on October 28, 1992, were certainly not the first to set a date, for date-setting endeavors have persisted throughout the centuries. While some date setters have been honest persons with good intentions, others have been unscrupulous, gain-seeking individuals.

From the beginning of the twentieth century there have been a number of prognosticators, or self-pronounced prophets, predicting some version of the end of the world. Sadly, the victims of October, 1992, were neither the first nor the last to suffer from false predictions.

From the time that Jesus promised to come again, many have lived in constant expectation of His return. Paul made an attempt to calm the immediate expectation by writing: "Now we beseech you, brethren, by the coming of our Lord Jesus Christ. . . . That ye be not soon shaken in mind, or be troubled . . . as that the day of Christ is at hand. Let no man deceive you by any means: for that day shall not come, except there come a falling away first, and that man of sin be revealed, the son of perdition" (2 Thessalonians 2:1–3). In spite of this admonition, the early Christian's hope of an immediate return by Christ in their day persisted. This belief grew stronger as the years passed. Finally, attempts were made to pinpoint the exact year of our Lord's return. One of the first recorded date predictions was made by Hippolytus, bishop of Portus Romanus, who lived in the second and third centuries. Hippolytus actually set the time for the end of the world to take place around A.D. 500.[1]

A tutor of Constantine's son, by the name of

Lactantius, placed the advent about two hundred years from his day, or about A.D. 500.[2] Augustine himself had a concept that the millennium began with the first advent of Christ.[3] Later, in about the last decade of the sixth century, Pope Gregory expressed his conviction that the end of the world was at hand.[4] Beatus, a priest of Libana who lived in the eighth century, is said to have predicted the exact date of the judgment. His followers waited from Easter Saturday evening to the afternoon of Easter Sunday.[5] Through the influence of Origen, who attempted to spiritualize the resurrection, and Eusebius, who allegorically interpreted the scriptures by stating that the established earthly church fulfilled the prophecies of the kingdom, date setting continued to persist.[6] St. Augustine's interpretation of the millennium beginning at the birth of Christ took on new emphasis in the year A.D.1000. St. Augustine's doctrine created no small stir and a great interest took hold of Europe concerning the Advent. "The pulpits loudly resounded with it."[7] Waddington also mentions a hermit from Thuringia, who thought, on the basis of a supposed special revelation from God, that at the end of the thousand years, Satan's chains would be broken and the world would be consumed.

The hermit was not alone in his declarations. Many others began to swell the alarm, until the teaching excited terror. Great numbers gave themselves to the service of the church hoping for merit. Others surrendered their properties to the churches and monasteries. Some journeyed to Palestine to meet Christ.[8] However, the catastrophe never arrived. The terrorized people returned to sobriety. But the organization that benefited from the failed *parousia* was the church, "which was enriched by the donations inspired by the impending day of doom."[9] During the Medieval Ages an Italian monk who lived around the twelfth century named Joachim of Flores, became a great expounder of prophecy. He also set a year for the coming of the Lord. His date was the year 1260. However, as with the others, the expected day never materialized.[10] As the Reformation era dawned, some of its leaders had a growing conviction that the end was approaching in their day. Among those who attempted to set dates was John Milicz of Kaomeriz, precursor of the Bohemian John Huss, who set the year around 1367. Arnold, a physician of Villanova, France, c. 1235–1313, declared the advent around 1373.[11] Wycliffe of England, who published his work, *The Last Age of the Chirche*, in 1356, taught that the judgment was at hand.[12] Even Christopher Columbus, the explorer, joined his voice to the chorus of prognosticators. In 1502 he completed his book, *Libro de las Profecias*. In it he predicted the end of the world in 1652.

The obsession for time setting continued through the Reformation era. Most of the date setters were motivated by their beliefs that the church was corrupt; the pope was the spirit of Antichrist, and that the church must be purified. It would probably be impossible to list all of the dates that were set, but they included 1528, 1533, and 1535, among others. During those years a Michael Steifel of Esslinger even set a time for the actual day and hour of Christ's coming. Unfortunately for him, his followers punished him when the appointed time came and went without the expected event.[13] Later the inventor of logarithms, John Napier (1550–1617), predicted that 1700 would be the year.[14] Another scientist and philosopher, Sir Isaac Newton (1642–1727), also entered the arena of prophetic interpretation and affirmed that the last age was approaching. In Germany a professor of Divinity at Denkendorf, named Albrecht Bengel (1687–1750) of Stuttgart, accepted the belief of the nearness of the Second Coming and concluded that it would take place in 1836. As a result, he wrote much on the speedy return of Christ, and preached it. Other prominent eighteenth-century heralds of the end time included:

- Johann Wilhelm, (d. 1727) and K. R. Hagenbach.[15]
- Johann Philipp Petri, (1718–1792), who dated the coming in 1847.[16]
- John Gill, a Baptist expositor and Orientalist (1697–1771), who looked for the end of the reign of Antichrist in 1866.
- Hans Wood (d.c. 1803) of Rosemead,

Ireland, who deduced that the end would come in 1880. Cited in Froom.[17]

The prophetic preaching also spanned the Atlantic Ocean, reaching the shores of America. In fact, during this time there were literally scores of clerics writing and expounding on Bible prophecy and the soon return of Christ. Prominent American ministers who espoused the soon-coming end of the world included:

- Thomas Parker (1595–1677), a pioneer Congregationalist minister of Massachusetts, anticipated the end of the world in 1859.
- Daniel T. Taylor.[18]
- Joseph Wolff, who wielded a widespread influence and traveled extensively throughout the British Isles, parts of Europe, Africa and India, before finally making his way to the United States. Believing that the Lord would appear and set up His kingdom in 1847, he preached with great enthusiasm Joseph Wolff was even granted an audience before the U.S. Congress and the clergy in Washington, D.C. He also went before the Legislatures of New Jersey and Pennsylvania.

Most of the prognosticators during the nineteenth century set the end of time somewhere between 1866 and 1900.[19] However, the idea gathered momentum in the decade of the 1830s. It was the conversion of a farmer named William Miller to Christianity that catapulted the belief of the imminent return of Jesus even further into the public eye. William Miller, who announced that the world would end about the year 1843, created no small stir among the populace with his preaching. Thousands gathered in his tent, or crowded rented halls to hear him expound on his prophetic interpretations.

Miller finally sharpened his calculations and announced that the advent would occur and the sanctuary (which he believed to be the earth) purified sometime between March 21, 1843, and March 21, 1844. Miller later accepted the date October 22, 1844.[20] Thousands accepted his calculations, and many, as in the year 1000, left their crops ungathered, gave up their lands and abandoned their homes as they excitedly anticipated the return of their Lord.

The morning of October 22 found hundreds gathered in different parts of the country. But as the day wore on, the waiting ones grew anxious. Finally the sun set—and they had to face the fact that October 22 had passed uneventfully. With shattered hopes and unable to explain the delay, some attempted to reset the date. Meanwhile, the caviling and mockery of the disappointed and despairing believers by the media was unmerciful. Sadly, some of the most ardent supporters and believers became the worst critics and opponents of the movement. Consequently, the movement sank into disgrace and dissipated, leaving as a remnant, a few diehards who persisted on futilely resetting dates.

It was from one of these groups that Pastor Charles Russell, the founder of the Watchtower Society of Jehovah's Witnesses, accepted the teaching that Christ would return in 1874. They calculated that it would be exactly thirty years after the "Great Disappointment" of October 22, 1844. When nothing happened on the predicted date, Russell explained to his followers that Christ did come on that date, but it was in secret; only those with spiritual sight had been able to see Him. In July 1879, he began to promulgate this new teaching in a paper entitled, "Zion's Watchtower and Herald of Christ's Presence." He also set 1914 for the end of the world.[21] When the end did not come in 1914, and World War I had broken out in that year, Russell's successor, Judge Rutherford moved the time of Christ's invisible coming to that date.

In the book *The Finished Mystery*, page 485, it was foretold that God would destroy in 1918 "the churches wholesale and the church members by millions." On page 258 it had stated that "the republics will disappear in the fall of 1920." However, Rutherford is best remembered for having set 1925 as the date for the setting up of the kingdom with the resurrection of Abraham, Isaac, and Jacob, and so forth. Although they failed to appear as he predicted, he still had the mansion "Beth-Sarim" built in San Diego, California, for them to occupy on their return. But it was he who occupied it and enjoyed a very lavish lifestyle there until his death in 1942.[22]

After the failure of these dates the Jehovah's Witnesses stated in 1931 that they had "learned to quit fixing dates for the future."[23] However, in 1966 they launched another aggressive campaign suggesting that 6,000 years of man's existence on earth would climax in the year 1975.[24] Once more the predicted year passed, an event which turned out to be a great fiasco for the Society, and a devastation for thousands of its members. See ibid., p.16.

The preceding examples clearly demonstrate the disastrous results of date setting. The constant parade of date-setting predictions have served as inoculations rather than an inspiration, and have tended to render their victims immune to future warnings and dangers.

Unfortunately, movements exist even at the present time suggesting that the world will end on this or that date. Some rely on chronological calculations to establish that the earth is supposed to last only six thousand years and set their date. But the wisest manner to deal with the time of Jesus' coming is to accept what He tells us in His Word. He said, "But of that day and hour knoweth no man, no, not the angels of heaven, but my Father only" (Matthew 24:36). And the best posture is to, "Keep yourselves in the love of God, looking for the mercy of our Lord Jesus Christ unto eternal life" (Jude 1:21).

For Some of Us, it Might as Well Be Today.

Thank the Lord, we are safe!" Those were the first words that proceeded out of my wife's mouth as soon as our car came to a halt. We had been traveling at about sixty miles an hour when our car suddenly swerved out of control and went rocketing off the highway. After the fact, we discovered we had hit black ice on the pavement, which explained why our trailer was suddenly sitting beside us instead of behind us! We were moving in a different direction than we intended, leaving us at last on a pile of snow in the vast, open lands of Wyoming.

No one is ever prepared for an accident. They happen so suddenly—so swiftly—that you do not even know what has happened until after the fact.

The same used to be true of natural catastrophes: no one was ever ready. However, modern technology now allows us to "foresee" a good deal of the weather, thereby avoiding some of its devastating consequences. This is especially true when it comes to hurricanes or other trackable storms.

However, no modern instrument will ever be able to alert us concerning the advent of Christ. No radio or television news flash will forewarn, no newspaper headline will report, no breaking of a code will anticipate that glorious event. In spite of the surprise nature of our Lord's coming, it will not be an accident. No, this event has been well planned in advance. It has been strategically mapped out, and all heaven waits with eager anticipation for its fulfillment. Nevertheless, just like an accident, it will be so sudden that the realization of what took place will become obvious after the fact.

Of course, that actual eventful hour remains a locked secret, for Jesus Himself stated that "of that day and hour knoweth no man, no, not the angels of heaven, but my Father only" (Matthew 24:36).

Inasmuch as no one can calculate the exact day or hour, the remedy for its reception lies in our vigilance. Calling attention to the need for being alert, Jesus said, "Take ye heed, watch and pray: for ye know not when the time is. For the Son of man is as a man taking a far journey, who left his house, and gave authority to his servants, and to every man his work, and commanded the porter to watch. Watch ye therefore: for ye know not when the master of the house cometh, at even, or at midnight, or at the cock crowing, or in the morning: lest coming suddenly he find you sleeping. And what I say unto you I say to all, Watch" (Mark 13:33–37).

Jesus warns us again in the book of Luke,

telling us to "take heed to yourselves, lest at any time your hearts be overcharged with surfeiting, and drunkenness, and cares of this life, and so that day come upon you unawares. For as a snare shall it come on all them that dwell on the face of the whole earth. Watch ye therefore, and pray always, that ye may be accounted worthy to escape all these things that shall come to pass, and to stand before the Son of man" (Luke 21:34–36).

To illustrate the suddenness of the Second Coming, Jesus said, "As the lightning cometh out of the east, and shineth even unto the west; so shall also the coming of the Son of man be" (Matthew 24:27). Lightning is associated with velocity and visibility. It flashes without warning—yet it is seen. It also strikes with such amazing and surprising speed that, though the effects are eternally lasting, its presence is just for an instant—which is why Jesus cautioned His followers to "watch therefore, for ye know neither the day nor the hour wherein the Son of man cometh" (Matthew 25:13). Notice He did not say month, year, or decade, but rather day, or hour.

The swiftness of Christ's coming is given further attention by the apostles Paul, Peter, John, and others. In Romans 9:28 Paul explains that, "he [Jesus] will finish the work, and cut it short in righteousness: because *a short work* will the Lord make upon the earth." Paul addressed the topic again in his letter to the Thessalonians, warning that "when they shall say, Peace and safety; then *sudden destruction* cometh upon them, as travail upon a woman with child; and they shall not escape" (1 Thessalonians 5:3).

Peter cautioned the believers that "the day of the Lord will come *as a thief in the night*; in the which the heavens shall pass away with a great noise, and the elements shall melt with fervent heat, the earth also and the works that are therein shall be burned up" (2 Peter 3:10).

And, finally, in the last book of Holy Writ, Jesus says, "Remember therefore how thou hast received and heard, and hold fast, and repent. If therefore thou shalt not watch, I will come on thee *as a thief*, and *thou shalt not know what hour* I will come upon thee" and again, "Behold, *I come quickly*; and my reward is with me, to give every man according as his work shall be" (Revelation 3:3; 22:12).

Yes, we are promised that the coming of our Lord will happen swiftly—and unexpectedly—as the approach of a thief in the night, or the start of labor for a woman with child. There will be no time to prepare for it then, which is why it is so important for each of us to be ready **now**.

"And what I say unto you I say to all, Watch" (Mark 13:37).

But What About "False Starts?"

If you have heard about the long history of false starts and date setting regarding the second coming of Christ, you might be wondering "Why rush about to get ready anyway?" or "Haven't people been preaching for centuries that Jesus would be coming, and yet He has not come?"

These are good questions and they merit an answer. The predictions of the second coming of Christ are not a modern-day phenomenon. The message of a Second Coming with its attending urgency has been heralded for centuries and even millenniums. In the book of Jude we read the following passage: "And Enoch also, the seventh from Adam, prophesied of these, saying, Behold, the Lord cometh with ten thousands of his saints, to execute judgment upon all, and to convince all that are ungodly among them of all their ungodly deeds which they have ungodly committed, and of all their hard speeches which ungodly sinners have spoken against him" (Jude 1:14–15).

It is indisputable that the belief of the speedy return of our Lord has been around for quite awhile. In fact, over five thousand years have expired since the time Enoch gave his prediction of Christ's coming as recorded in the book of Jude.

Yet does this mean that Christ will never come? No! That there has been a great delay is evident. However, concerning this apparent delay Peter writes, "Knowing this first, that there shall come in the last days scoffers, walking after their own lusts, and saying, Where is the promise of his coming? for since the fathers fell asleep, all things continue as they were from the beginning of the creation. For this they willingly are ignorant of, that by the word of God the heavens were of old, and the earth standing out of the water and in the water: whereby the world that then was, being overflowed with water, perished: but the heavens and the earth, which are now, by the same word are kept in store, reserved unto fire against the day of judgment and perdition of ungodly men. But, beloved, be not ignorant of this one thing, that one day is with the Lord as a thousand years, and a thousand years as one day" (2 Peter 3:3–8).

Evidently, our heavenly Father knew that there would be a great lapse of time—even millenniums—between the giving of the prophecies and Christ's second coming. Why then the rush to get ready? What is the hurry? Why the urgency?

First of all, I do not believe that our Lord gave the warning with such pressing urgency without a very good reason. God is not seeking to put us all on alert just for the fun of it. Neither is He playing with His children by building up their hopes only to have them disappointed, shattered, or to cause them to suffer disillusionment. No, I believe that there are several reasons for the constant emphasis on the imminent return of Christ.

The first reason is man's life expectancy. There is not one of us who lives the duration of a millennium. The scripture says that man's pilgrimage on the earth is compared to the grass that is here today, but withers tomorrow. Most of us can expect to be around, even barring accident, and, if health should permit, for no longer than eighty to ninety years. Some may, by reason of strength, last until one hundred years of age or a little beyond. But none of us has the luxury of waiting beyond our allotted time to prepare ourselves for eternity. As a result, any decision made relative to our salvation must be accomplished during our short life span.

This leads us to the next point—the uncertainty of life itself. We are not promised tomorrow. In fact, we can never be sure even of today. Life is so full of surprises! There are those who are fortunate to live out their full tenure. Yet we are constantly reminded by the disasters, calamities, and catastrophes around us of the fragility of life. If this was a matter of concern in times past, it certainly should be of greater concern today. We may have our lives snuffed out by some stray bullet or the sudden touchdown of a tornado, while sitting in our own living room.

It could be by some unheard of disaster—by land, air, or sea. We dwell in a time when strange things are taking place. Millions fled from the fear of death in Rwanda only to meet death by plague in their newly-found refuge of Congo.

Death is no respecter of age or person. It can come "knocking at the door" when least expected. It is for this reason that Paul says, "Knowing the time, that now it is high time to awake out of sleep: for now is our salvation nearer than when we believed. The night is far spent, the day is at hand: let us therefore cast off the works of darkness, and let us put on the armour of light." Again He said, "For he saith, I have heard thee in a time accepted, and in the day of salvation have I succored thee: behold, now is the accepted time; behold, now is the day of salvation" (Romans 13:11–12: 2 Corinthians 6:2).

The parable of the rich man and Lazarus in Luke 16:19–31 was given to sound the same warning. It was not given to teach that the righteous spend eternity in the "bosom of Abraham," for that is not the eternal habitation of the saved—neither is Abraham our Saviour. It was not given to teach that the wicked spend ceaseless ages being tormented in hell; or that a drop of water on the tongue (which the rich man asked for in the parable) could ever quench the thirst of one suffering such torturing heat. This parable was given to make clear that there is a "great gulf fixed" between the dead and the living (verse 26).

Plainly stated, death seals our destiny. Whatever we fail to accomplish while we are living can never be altered after death. It is because of this fact that God calls us always to be ready, for if our lives are in a constant state of readiness, and death should take us unexpectedly, our salvation will be sure.

We cannot afford to put off our preparation. It is while we are alive that the choice must be made. Every day affords us another opportunity to accept or reject God's invitation for salvation. The choice we make in this life will be our choice for all eternity. We shall receive either eternal life or eternal death. We are called upon to overcome in this life as Christ overcame. Heaven has provided us with abundant opportunities and privileges so that we can be victorious over sin just as Christ was victorious over sin. And for this cause, ample opportunity is provided while life lasts.

Another thought to ponder is the perceived brevity of time between death and the Second Coming. In other words, if a person dies secure in the Lord, time is of no consequence. When awakened in that glorious resurrection day, the person will not have been aware of the passing of time. Centuries or millenniums will have fled away like moments. In one moment they died, and in the next moment they awaken to behold their Lord descending from heaven to rescue them.

The Bible compares death to a sleep (see John 11:14; 1 Thessalonians 4:13–17). It also states that "the living know that they shall die: but the dead know not any thing, neither have they any more a reward; for the memory of them is forgotten. Also their love, and their hatred, and their envy, is now perished; neither have they any more a portion for ever in any thing that is done under the sun" (Ecclesiastes 9:5–6). Therefore, in the unconscious state of death, or sleep, one is not cognizant of what is transpiring. Thus for all practical purposes, when our life ends, and the advent finally arrives, it will be for us as though we had taken a brief nap.

One more thought concerning the need to be ever ready, is that of our witness. There are millions who, in spite of our ability to communicate through modern technology, have never heard of the gospel, nor are they even aware that the Lord is coming. As a consequence, they are not knowledgeable concerning the need to prepare for eternity during this probationary time of life. There are multitudes in this condition—sadly unprepared to face their eternal destiny.

For many of them, perhaps the only opportunity they will ever have to become aware of it is by coming in contact with those whose consistent Christian lives give evidence that there is a heaven to gain and a hell to shun. An excited, loving, and patiently-waiting Christian is the best advertisement for the belief of a soon-coming Saviour. This state of constant readiness contributes to keeping the believer focused on the priorities of life. This in turn can aid in reorienting onlookers who are searching for hope in our troubled world.

There is yet another reason why we should be ever ready for our Lord's return—the reason that I believe is the most important—our own longing for Jesus to come. When you love people, you want to be with them. And our Saviour is no exception. He longs to be with us, His children, just as a parent would be anxious to be with their distant and separated loved ones.

Consider how much time has transpired since Jesus said, "I will come again." Imagine how He must yearn to come and gather to Himself His own! But this longing must be reciprocal. We too must desire to be with Him!

In order to encourage a cultivation of this longing, Paul wrote to Titus, "Looking for that blessed hope, and the glorious appearing of the great God and our Saviour Jesus Christ" (Titus 2:13). In addressing the Hebrews he repeated the same encouragement: "So Christ was once offered to bear the sins of many; and unto them that look for him shall he appear the second time without sin unto salvation" (Hebrews 9:28).

This theme—this longing for Jesus to come—was constantly shared among all the believers. It was this hope that gave strength to the aged apostle, who, while facing death, wrote, "For our conversation is in heaven; from whence also we look for the Saviour, the Lord Jesus Christ" (Philippians 3:20). Yes, we ought to love our blessed Lord so much that we will work and pray, doing all we can to hasten His appearing.

Those who have this blessed hope in their hearts will be affected by it. "Beloved," John wrote, "now are we the sons of God, and it doth not yet appear what we shall be: but we know that, when he shall appear, we shall be like him; for we shall see him as he is. And every man that hath this hope in him purifieth himself, even as he is pure" (1 John 3:2–3).

And what a privilege is afforded us through the gospel. As believers, we may not only hope to see Him when He comes, but we may abide with Him now. In the beautiful words of John, "And now, little children, abide in him; that, when he shall appear, we may have confidence, and not be ashamed before him at his coming" (1 John 2:28).

[1] Phillip Schaff, ed., *Ante-Nicene Christianity*, pp. 769–770, cited in LeRoy Edwin Froom, *Faith of Our Fathers*, I, chap. 9.
[2] Lactantius, *The Divine Institutes*, book VII, chap. 25, ibid., VII 220.
[3] Phillip Schaff, *History of the Christian Church*, II, 122.
[4] James Robertson, *History of the Christian Church*, II, 369–370, 378.
[5] Augustus Neander, *General History of the Christian Religion and Church*, III, 163–164, cited in Charles Elliot Weniger, *A Cultural Analysis and Appraisal of the Public Address of William Miller*, p. 18, May, 1946.
[6] Phillip Schaff, *History of the Christian Church*, II, 122; Eusebius, *Church History, Life of Constantine the Great, Oration in Praise of Constantine*, Henry Wace and Phillip Schaff, editors, *A Select Library of Nicene and Post Nicene Fathers of the Christian Churches*, Second Series, I; Aurelius Augustinus, *The City of God*, Book XVII, chap. 53.
[7] George Waddington, *A History of the Church from the Earliest Ages to the Reformation*, pp. 223–224.
[8] John Lawrence Von Mosheim, *Institutes of Ecclesiastical History*, II, pp. 130–131.
[9] Elmer T. Clark, *The Small Sects in America*, p. 39; Waddington, op. cit., p. 224.
[10] Shirley Jackson Case, *The Millennial Hope*, p. 184.
[11] Froom, op. cit., II, pp. 71–72.
[12] Ibid., pp. 58–59.
[13] Ibid., pp. 320–322.
[14] Ibid., pp. 455–458.
[15] *A Text Book of the History of Doctrines*, II, 370–371.
[16] Froom, op. cit., 713–719.
[17] op. cit.
[18] *The Reign of Christ on Earth*, p. 302.
[19] Froom, op. cit., pp. 338–346, 396–484.
[20] Joshua V. Himes, *Apology and Defense*, p.12.
[21] Watchtower Society, *Millennial Dawn*, vol. 2, pp. 76–78.
[22] E. B. Price, *Our Friends The Jehovah's Witnesses*, p. 15; E. B. Price, *God's Channel of Truth, Is It the Watch Tower?*, p. 30.
[23] E. B. Price, *Our Friends the Jehovah's Witnesses*, pp.16–17.
[24] Watchtower Society, *Life Everlasting—In Freedom of the Sons of God*, p. 26, cited in, E.B. Price, *Our Friends the Jehovah's Witnesses*, p. 17.

6

What Will Happen When He Comes?

The Righteous and the Wicked Will Have Two Very Different Destinies

Because of the widespread confusion concerning who will be affected by the coming of the Lord, and how they will be affected, it is imperative to compare the texts describing this eventful scenario.

In order for us to get the whole picture concerning what will be occurring at the Second Coming—what is happening to the righteous and the wicked—it is necessary to look at the texts which specifically apply to each respective group.

Destiny of the Saved

Matthew 24:31: "And he shall send his angels with a great sound of a trumpet, and they shall gather together his elect from the four winds, from one end of heaven to the other."

Matthew 25:31, 34: "When the Son of man shall come in his glory, and all the holy angels with him, then shall he sit upon the throne of his glory. . . . Then shall the King say unto them on his right hand, Come, ye blessed of my Father, inherit the kingdom prepared for you from the foundation of the world."

Mark 13:26–27: "And then shall they see the Son of man coming in the clouds with great power and glory. And then shall he send his angels, and shall gather together his elect from the four winds, from the uttermost part of the earth to the uttermost part of heaven."

1 Thessalonians 4:13–18: "But I would not have you to be ignorant, brethren, concerning them which are asleep, that ye sorrow not, even as others which have no hope. For if we believe that Jesus died and rose again, even so them also which sleep in Jesus will God bring with him. For this we say unto you by the word of the Lord, that we which are alive and remain unto the coming of the Lord shall not

prevent them which are asleep. For the Lord himself shall descend from heaven with a shout, with the voice of the archangel, and with the trump of God: and the dead in Christ shall rise first: then we which are alive and remain shall be caught up together with them in the clouds, to meet the Lord in the air: and so shall we ever be with the Lord."

John 6:40: "And this is the will of him that sent me, that every one which seeth the Son, and believeth on him, may have everlasting life: and I will raise him up at the last day."

1 Corinthians 15:23, 51–54: "But every man in his own order: Christ the firstfruits; afterward they that are Christ's at his coming. . . . Behold, I shew you a mystery; we shall not all sleep, but we shall all be changed, in a moment, in the twinkling of an eye, at the last trump: for the trumpet shall sound, and the dead shall be raised incorruptible, and we shall be changed. For this corruptible must put on incorruption, and this mortal must put on immortality. So when this corruptible shall have put on incorruption, and this mortal shall have put on immortality, then shall be brought to pass the saying that is written, Death is swallowed up in victory."

Revelation 20:6: "Blessed and holy is he that hath part in the first resurrection: on such the second death hath no power, but they shall be priests of God and of Christ, and shall reign with him a thousand years."

John 14:1–3: "Let not your heart be troubled: ye believe in God, believe also in me. In my Father's house are many mansions: if it were not so, I would have told you. I go to prepare a place for you. And if I go and prepare a place for you, I will come again, and receive you unto myself; that where I am, there ye may be also."

Fate of the Unsaved

Matthew 13:40–42: "As therefore the tares are gathered and burned in the fire; so shall it in the end of this world. The Son of man shall send forth his angels, and they shall gather out of his kingdom all things that offend, and them which do iniquity; and shall cast them into a furnace of fire: there shall be wailing and gnashing of teeth."

Matthew 13:49–50: "So shall it be at the end of the world: the angels shall come forth, and sever the wicked from among the just, and shall cast them into the furnace of fire: there shall be wailing and gnashing of teeth."

Matthew 24:30: "And then shall appear the sign of the Son of man in heaven: and then shall all the tribes of the earth mourn, and they shall see the Son of man coming in the clouds of heaven with power and great glory."

Matthew 24:37–39: "But as the days of Noe were, so shall also the coming of the Son of man be. For as in the days that were before the flood they were eating and drinking, marrying and giving in marriage, until the day Noe entered into the ark, and knew not until the flood came, and took them all away; so shall also the coming of the Son of man be."

Luke 17:26–30, 34, 37: "And as it was in the days of Noe, so shall it be also in the days of the Son of man. They did eat, they drank, they married wives, they were given in marriage, until the day that Noe entered into the ark, and the flood came, and destroyed them all. Likewise also as it was in the days of Lot; they did eat, they drank, they bought, they sold, they planted, they builded; but the same day that Lot went out of Sodom it rained fire and brimstone from heaven, and destroyed them all. Even thus shall it be in the day when the Son of man is revealed. . . . I tell you, in that night there shall be two in one bed; the one shall be taken, and the other shall be left. . . and they answered and said unto him, Where, Lord? And he said unto them, Wheresoever the body is, thither will the eagles be gathered together."

2 Thessalonians 1:6–9: "Seeing it is a righteous thing with God to recompense tribulation to them that trouble you; and to you who are troubled rest with us, when the Lord Jesus shall be revealed from heaven with his mighty angels, in flaming fire taking vengeance on them that know not God, and that obey not the gospel of our Lord Jesus Christ: who shall be punished with everlasting destruction from the presence of the Lord, and from the glory of his power."

2 Thessalonians 2:8: "Then shall that Wicked be revealed, whom the Lord shall consume with the spirit of his mouth, and shall destroy with the brightness of his coming."

Jude 1:14–15: "And Enoch also, the seventh from Adam, prophesied of these, saying, Behold, the Lord cometh with ten thousands of his saints, to execute judgment upon all, and to convince all that are ungodly among them of all their ungodly deeds which they have ungodly committed, and of all their hard speeches which ungodly sinners have spoken against him."

Revelation 6:15–17: "And the kings of the earth, and the great men, and the rich men, and the chief captains, and the mighty men, and every bondman, and every free man, hid themselves in the dens and in the rocks of the mountains; and said to the mountains and rocks, Fall on us, and hide us from the face of him that sitteth on the throne, and from the wrath of the Lamb: for the great day of his wrath is come; and who shall be able to stand?"

Revelation 19:11, 14, 20–21: "And I saw heaven opened, and behold a white horse; and he that sat upon him was called Faithful and True, and in righteousness he doth judge and make war. . . . And the armies which were in heaven followed him upon white horses, clothed in fine linen, white and clean. . . . And the beast was taken, and with him the false prophet that wrought miracles before him, with which he deceived them that had received the mark of the beast, and them that worshipped his image. These both were cast alive into a lake of fire burning with brimstone. And the remnant were slain with the sword of him that sat upon the horse, which sword proceeded out of his mouth: and all the fowls were filled with their flesh."

Revelation 20:1–2, 5: "And I saw an angel come down from heaven, having the key of the bottomless pit and a great chain in his hand. And he laid hold on the dragon, that old serpent, which is the Devil, and Satan, and bound him a thousand years. . . . But the rest of the dead lived not again until the thousand years were finished. This is the first resurrection."

In reviewing the texts describing the two comparative groups we realize there are several scenes transpiring almost simultaneously. Notice the following points:

1. Christ comes as a Conqueror—with power and great glory. His appearance is visible, for He is revealed. See Matthew 25:31; Mark 13:26; Acts 1:9–11; 2 Thessalonians 1:7; Revelation 1:7.

2.The angels, which the Bible refers to as the "saints" or "armies of heaven," come with Jesus. See Matthew 25:31; Mark 13:27; Jude 1:14–15; Revelation 19:14.

3. They (the angels) bring attention to His appearance by the sounding of their trumpets. Thus, we can be sure that the Second Coming will be heard. See Matthew 24:31; 1 Thessalonians 4:16; 1 Corinthians 15:52.

4. The heavens are affected by the magnitude of Christ's coming, and the earth begins to heave and reel. See Isaiah 24:18–22; Revelation 6:14; 2 Peter 3:10.

5. The wicked see Him and begin to seek refuge in the rocks and mountains. See Matthew 24:30; Revelation 1:7; Revelation 6:15–17.

6. The righteous dead are resurrected, changed, and lifted up from the earth. See 1 Corinthians 15:23, 51–58; 1 Thessalonians 4:13–16; Revelation 20:6.

7. The righteous living are changed (without experiencing death), and are also lifted up from the earth. See 1 Corinthians 15:51–52; 1 Thessalonians 4:17.

8. The wicked are destroyed. See 2 Thessalonians 2:8; Luke 17:37; 2 Thessalonians 1:8–9; Revelation 19:20–21; Isaiah 24:18–22.

9. The wicked, who have been dead prior to this event, remain dead until the second and final resurrection. See Revelation 20:5.

10. The devil is apprehended and placed in detention for 1000 years. See Revelation 20:1–2.

11. The Lord returns to heaven with all the righteous. See John 14:1–3; Revelation 20:6; 1 Thessalonians 4:17.

12. The earth is left in ruin and desolation. See Jeremiah 4:23–26; Revelation 20:1–2; Revelation 19:21.

In reading these verses, it is clear that there will be two tangible groups cohabiting together at the time of Christ's second advent. Each will have their particular experience in that day. They are dwelling together now, but at the appearance of Christ they will be divided.

This physical division between the two classes will be done by the Lord Himself. Referring to it, Jesus said, "When the Son of man shall come in his glory, and all the holy angels with him, then shall he sit upon the throne of his glory: and before him shall be gathered all nations: and he shall separate them one from another, as a shepherd divideth his sheep from the goats; and he shall set the sheep on his right hand, but the goats on the left" (Matthew 25:31–33).

In Matthew 13:24–30, this segregating is further illustrated by the parable of the wheat and the tares. In response to the disciples' request to "declare unto us the parable of the tares of the field" (Matthew 13:36), "He [Jesus] answered and said unto them, He that soweth the good seed is the Son of man; the field is the world; the good seed are the children of the kingdom; but the tares are the children of the wicked one; the enemy that sowed them is the devil; the harvest is the end of the world; and the reapers are the angels. As therefore the tares are gathered and burned in the fire; so shall it be in the end of this world. The Son of man shall send forth his angels, and they shall gather out of his kingdom all things that offend, and them which do iniquity; and shall cast them into a furnace of fire: there shall be wailing and gnashing of teeth. Then shall the righteous shine forth as the sun in the kingdom of their Father. Who hath ears to hear, let him hear" (Matthew 13:37–43).

In verses 47–50 of the same chapter the separation is compared to fish being caught and divided. The same concept is supported by the slumbering virgins of Matthew 25:1–12, who were awakened by the announcement of the bridegroom's appearance, and were separated into two groups: the wise and the foolish virgins. Other Bible examples of the separation of the righteous and wicked include: Noah and the antediluvians (Matthew 24:37–39); Lot and the Sodomites (Luke

17:28–30), and those who claim, "Lord, Lord," but find rejection in Matthew 7:21–23.

Think of it! What inexpressible joy will be experienced in that day by those who have availed themselves of every provision made by Heaven for their preparation. And what deep regret, anguish of heart and terror, will be experienced by those who could have been on the right side. Too late they have realized the glorious opportunity they allowed to pass by—too late will reality dawn: Jesus did come, but they were not ready.

The Angels Will Gather the Saints

When Jesus comes, as already stated, He will not mysteriously take a part of His children and return later for the third time to gather the rest. He will take His bride as a complete whole, the living as well as those who have died.

Concerning those who have passed away, we read, "For the Lord himself shall descend from heaven with a shout, with the voice of the archangel, and with the trump of God; and the dead in Christ shall rise first" (1 Thessalonians 4:16).

The dead in Christ, those who died believing in Him, will rise first. Just imagine that day. The ground begins to shake; it is not able to contain the dead any longer. Jesus says, "Awake and sing, ye that dwell in the dust: for thy dew is as the dew of herbs, and the earth shall cast out the dead" (Isaiah 26:19).

Suddenly, like Lazarus of old who had been dead for four days, they begin to come out of the ground. Some have been dead for decades, others for centuries, and still others for millenniums. They are awakening to the newness of life, fresh with the vigor of youth. Sickness and disease are gone. Their deformities are transformed. They are changed into immortality "in a moment, in the twinkling of an eye, at the last trump: for the trumpet shall sound, and the dead shall be raised incorruptible, and we shall be changed" (1 Corinthians 15:52).

They will come back to life in a renewed state, for God has promised that He "shall wipe away all tears from their eyes; and there shall be no more death, neither sorrow, nor crying, neither shall there be any more pain: for the former things are passed away" (Revelation 21:4). Unlike Lazarus, who was raised and died again, these will be raised to everlasting life. I long for that day, don't you?

I was preaching a sermon in a funeral parlor one day, speaking of Lazarus' death and how Christ brought him back to life. Looking at the crowd I said, "Picture yourself standing there watching Jesus say, 'Lazarus, come forth!' "

With bated breath, you see this fellow who was dead for four days get up and walk out of the tomb. What would you have done if you had been there?" I asked. Someone in the audience replied, "I would have had a heart attack!"

"And why?" I asked. If you really were a true believer in Jesus and His power, you would not have been fearful or shocked. Instead, you would have rejoiced with exceeding great joy!

So likewise, if you are a believer in that glorious day when Jesus comes and the dead are raised, you will be filled with such joy and happiness that you will not be able to contain yourself. What a thrill that will be, to actually see and experience the reality of God's promise (that the dead in Christ shall rise), come true before your very eyes!

So, at His coming, as with exuberant joy you watch the dead rise, you also will rise. As Paul describes it, "Then we which are alive and remain shall be caught up together with them in the clouds, to meet the Lord in the air" (1 Thessalonians 4:17).

Yes, the dead in Christ who are resurrected, and those who are alive at His coming, will be caught up together to meet the Lord in the air simultaneously. This is the whole wonderful beauty of it, the whole purpose of redemption! In that glad day "he shall send his angels with a great sound of a trumpet, and they shall gather together his elect from the four winds, from one end of heaven to the other" (Matthew 24:31). Yes, He will gather all His children—those who have died, and those who are alive.

The Angels Do the Gathering

In Matthew 13:24–30, Jesus gives a parable describing the gathering. "Another parable put he forth unto them, saying, The kingdom of heaven is likened unto a man which sowed good seed in his field: but while men slept, his enemy came and sowed tares among the wheat, and went his way. But when the blade was sprung up, and brought forth fruit, then appeared the tares also. So the servants of the householder came and said unto him, Sir, didst not thou sow good seed in thy field? from whence then hath it tares? He said unto them, An enemy hath done this. The servants said unto him, Wilt thou then that we go and gather them up? But He said, Nay; lest while ye gather up the tares, ye root up also the wheat with them. Let both grow together until the harvest: and in the time of harvest I will say to the reapers, Gather ye together first the tares, and bind them in bundles to burn them: but gather the wheat into my barn."

The disciples of Jesus typically found His parables difficult to understand, and this one was no exception. So they came to Him privately, just as they always did, and asked the meaning of the parable.

"Then Jesus sent the multitude away, and went into the house: and his disciples came unto him, saying, Declare unto us the parable of the tares of the field. He answered and said unto them, He that soweth the good seed is the Son of man" (verse 36). The sower, then, represented Christ Himself.

"The field is the world" Jesus went on, and "the good seed are the children of the kingdom" (verse 37). In other words, those who love God and have accepted Him are called the children of the kingdom, or the good seed. In contrast, the "children of the wicked one" were the tares, and the enemy that sowed them is the devil. The harvest is the end of the world, and the reapers are the angels. "As therefore the tares are gathered and burned in the fire; so shall it be in the end of this world," Jesus explained (verse 40). He then concluded the parable with these words, "The Son of man shall send forth his angels, and they shall gather out of his kingdom all things that offend, and them which do iniquity; and shall cast them into a furnace of fire: there shall be wailing and gnashing of teeth. Then shall the righteous shine forth as the sun in the kingdom of their Father. Who hath ears to hear, let him hear" (Matthew 13:41–43).

The parable of the sower, then, gives us the sequence of separation in the last day. Through it we learn that Jesus plants the good seed, the devil plants the wicked seed, and both types of seed grow up together until the end of the world. When the harvest comes, the angels, or reapers, come and gather the tares first, and conclude with the gathering of the righteous. Both groups are gathered by the angels. Therefore, after their gathering, nothing remains on earth.

The angels of God have had an integral part to play in the salvation of mankind. Their ministry is recorded throughout the pages of Holy Writ. With intense interest they have interacted in the affairs of mortals, seeking to cooperate with God's plan to rescue man from eternal ruin. Their part in the final episodes of earth's history will be wrought with no less dedication.

Unfortunately, there are some who deny the clear Biblical statements concerning the involvement of the angelic host at Christ's second coming. Instead, they attempt to apply Jude 1:14 ("Behold, the Lord cometh with ten thousands of his saints") to "pre-raptured" saints or the spirits of the dead, rather than the angels of God. While at first glance this seems plausible, a careful comparison of Jude 1:14 yields the true picture.

The word "saints" used in Jude according to *Strong's Analytical Concordance*, is the Greek word "hagios." This word is translated 161 times as "Holy," 61 times as "Saints," 4 times as "Holy Ones," and 3 times in various other ways. Since the word means "holy," then arriving at the conclusion that these are human beings returning in spirit form from heaven to reconnect with their separated bodies, (as I heard a renowned preacher state on TV just the other day), is more in concert with Greek mythology or ancient pagan philosophy than with the Word of God.

The "Saints" in Jude 14 Are Angels

There are several references which make plain the meaning of Jude 1:14. The first is Deuteronomy 33:2, where Moses said, "The LORD came from Sinai, and rose up from Seir unto them; he shined forth from mount Paran, and he came with ten thousands of saints: from his right hand went a fiery law for them."

The second is Daniel 7:10, which states that "a fiery stream issued and came forth from before him: thousand thousands ministered unto him, and ten thousand times ten thousand stood before him: the judgment was set, and the books were opened."

In addition, Hebrews 12:22 declares: "Ye are come to mount Zion, and unto the city of the living God, the heavenly Jerusalem, and to an innumerable company of angels."

Judging from these texts we can see that:

1. The "Saints" cannot be New Testament returnees or departed human beings (as claimed by the rapturists), for there were no New Testament saints in the Old Testament.
2. The references to the ten thousands, and thousand thousands is obviously to an innumerable number of heavenly beings who have been with the Lord in the distant past, and shall attend Him in His return voyage in the near future. Finally,
3. Jesus never mentioned other beings except for the angels returning with Him.

Notice the following texts:

Matthew 13:41: "The Son of man shall send forth his angels, and they shall gather out of his kingdom all things that offend, and them which do iniquity."

Matthew 13:49: "So shall it be at the end of the world: the angels shall come forth, and sever [separate] the wicked from among the just [righteous]."

Matthew 16:27: "For the Son of man shall come in the glory of his Father with his angels; and then he shall reward every man according to his works."

Matthew 24:31: "And he shall send his angels with a great sound of a trumpet, and they shall gather his elect from the four winds, from one end of heaven to the other."

Matthew 25:31: "When the Son of man shall come in his glory, and all the holy angels with him, then shall he sit upon the throne of his glory."

Mark 8:38: "Whoever therefore shall be ashamed of me and of my words in this adulterous and sinful generation; of him also shall the Son of man be ashamed, when he cometh in the glory of his Father with the holy angels."

Mark 13:27: "And then he shall send his angels, and shall gather together his elect from the four winds, from the uttermost part of the earth to the uttermost part of heaven."

Luke 9:26: "For whoever shall be ashamed of me and of my words, of him shall the Son of man be ashamed, when he shall come in his own glory, and in his Father's, and of the holy angels."

1 Thessalonians 3:13: "To the end he may [e]stablish your hearts unblameable in holiness before God, even our Father, at the coming of our Lord Jesus Christ with all his saints." {saints: or, holy ones, or, angels}

2 Thessalonians 1:7: "And to you who are troubled rest with us, when the Lord Jesus shall be revealed from heaven with his mighty angels."

Revelation 19:14: "And the armies which were in heaven followed him upon white horses, clothed in fine linen, white and clean."

One can very quickly see from all of these related verses of scripture that Jesus did not intimate in the least that an innumerable company of humans would accompany Him on His return trip to the earth. On the contrary, it will be millions *of angels* who will come to participate in the greatest rescue mission of mankind ever undertaken!

The Wicked Will Be Taken to Destruction

> I tell you, in that night there shall be two men in one bed; the one shall be taken, and the other shall be left. Two women shall be grinding together; the one shall be taken, and the other left. Two men shall be in the field; the one shall be taken, and the other left" (Luke 17:34–36).

> "Then shall two be in the field; the one shall be taken, and the other left. Two women shall be grinding at the mill; the one shall be taken, and the other left" (Matthew 24:40–41).

A Likely Scenario?

The above texts are often quoted in support of the "secret rapture"—a worldwide event that many Christians believe will result in the disappearance of the righteous, who simply vanish or disappear, "taken" to heaven by the "rapture." In contrast, the wicked will be left behind for the "seven years of tribulation."

But do these texts saying "the one shall be taken and the other left" really support this common view of the rapture? While there are plenty of Christians who think so, there are others who disagree. Building their case on the Greek word for "take" (*paralambáno)*, this group concludes that the righteous are indeed "taken" to heaven, but those "left" behind are not left alive. In fact, these Christians would assert, and with plenty of Bible evidence, that it is the wicked—and not the righteous—who are "taken" at the second coming of Christ.

"Who" gets taken in these verses matters greatly, because the idea that the wicked (rather than the righteous) are "taken" undermines the whole theory of a rapture. For if the wicked are "taken," they obviously will not be around for the great "tribulation."

What the Bible Says

In considering these important questions, let us look more closely at the context of Matthew 24 and Luke 17 to determine what they actually teach:

> Matthew 24:37–41: "But as the days of Noe were, so shall also the coming of the Son of man be. For as in the days that were before the flood they were eating and drinking, marrying and giving in marriage, until the day that Noe entered into the ark . . . and took them all away; *so shall also* the coming of the Son of man be. Then shall two be in the field; the one shall be taken, and the other left. Two women shall be grinding at the mill; the one shall be taken, and the other left."

The context of the above passage actually conveys an overtaking, conquering, or destroying. In military terminology when a command is given to "take" a hill or a city, it means to overcome the defenders—take possession of it.

The same idea is conveyed in Joshua 11:12: "And all the cities of those kings, and all the kings of them, did Joshua **take**, and smote them with the edge of the sword, and he utterly destroyed them, as Moses the servant of the Lord commanded."

> Luke 17:22–37: "And he said unto the disciples, The days will come, when ye shall desire to see one of the days of the Son of man, and ye shall not see it. And they shall say to you, See here; or, see there: go not after them, nor follow them. For as the lightning, that lighteneth out of the one part under heaven, shineth unto the other

part under heaven; so shall also the Son of man be in his day. But first must he suffer many things, and be rejected of this generation. And as it was in the days of Noe, *so shall it be also* in the days of the Son of man. They did eat, they drank, they married wives, they were given in marriage, until the day that Noe entered into the ark, and the flood came, and destroyed them all. Likewise also as it was in the days of Lot; they did eat, they drank, they bought, they sold, they planted, they builded; but the same day that Lot went out of Sodom it rained fire and brimstone from heaven, and destroyed them all. Even thus shall it be in the day when the Son of man is revealed. In that day, he which shall be upon the housetop, and his stuff in the house, let him not come down to take it away: and he that is in the field, let him likewise not return back. Remember Lot's wife. Whosoever shall seek to save his life shall lose it; and whosoever shall lose his life shall preserve it. I tell you, in that night there shall be two men in one bed; the one shall be taken, and the other shall be left. Two women shall be grinding together; the one shall be taken, and the other left. Two men shall be in the field; the one shall be taken, and the other left. And they answered and said unto him, Where, Lord? And he said unto them, Wheresoever the body is, thither will the eagles be gathered together."

In considering the above verses, we can see without question that Jesus is telling His disciples what to expect at His advent. He compares conditions during both the Flood and the destruction of Sodom and Gomorrah to the end of time. We can also see that the phrases "so shall also" and "so shall it be also" pointed Christ's disciples to a replay. History is to have a rerun.

Focusing on the Wicked

When Jesus said, "As it was in the days of Noah," He was not addressing Noah's fate, nor that of the other seven in the ark. Rather, He was addressing the fate of those outside of the ark. Similarly, if you said "in the days of President Lincoln," the subject under consideration would not be President Lincoln himself, but something that happened during his time. Hence, the allusion of Jesus in the above verses constitutes a warning to unbelieving, unprepared future generations, who like those in Noah's day will be living when the "Son of man is revealed."

It must therefore be emphasized that it is the lost, the unbelievers, who are addressed in Matthew 24 and Luke 17. It is they who did not regard the warnings of impending doom. It is they who were "taken" in Noah's time—they who met with catastrophe. The believers were in the ark, safe in the refuge that, under God's direction, had been prepared for them. The fate of the survivors is not mentioned in Matthew 24 and Luke 17 because they are not the ones at issue.

Since it was those outside of the ark who were "taken" in Noah's time, and since Jesus states that the same circumstances would characterize His second coming, we may conclude that it will be the unbelievers who will be "taken" when He returns. And inasmuch as it was Noah who was left alive after the eradication of the earth's populace, it will be the righteous (those with a modern-day, Noah-like experience) who will be left—that survive and remain when the "Son of man" comes.

The very idea that the righteous were "taken" and the wicked left behind actually leaves those who believe in a rapture with a serious dilemma, for there is no Biblical end-time precedent for the idea that two groups (both the righteous and the wicked) remain alive. The wicked were destroyed in Noah's day, which was cited by Jesus as an example of what would happen at His coming. The wicked also met with destruction in Lot's day, which was also referred to by Jesus as an example of end-time events.

In other words, Jesus speaks of only two groups at His coming: one of which is left alive, while the other is "taken" to destruction. Speaking of those who will be taken, Peter writes, "The Lord knoweth how to deliver the godly out of temptations, and to reserve the unjust unto the day of judgment to be punished: But chiefly them that walk after the flesh in the lust of uncleanness, and despise government. Presumptuous [are they], selfwilled, they are not afraid to speak evil of dignities. Whereas angels, which are greater in power and might, bring not railing accusation against them before the Lord. But these, as natural brute beasts, made to ***be taken and destroyed,*** speak evil of the things that they understand not; and shall utterly perish in their own corruption; And shall receive the reward of unrighteousness, [as] they that count it pleasure to riot in the day time. 2 Peter 2: 9, 11-13.

The prophet Isaiah gives the following graphic description of that day: "Behold, the LORD maketh the earth empty, and maketh it waste, and turneth it upside down, and scattereth abroad the inhabitants thereof. And it shall be, as with the people, so with the priest; as with the servant, so with his master; as with the maid, so with her mistress; as with the buyer, so with the seller; as with the lender, so with the borrower; as with the taker of usury, so with the giver of usury to him. . . . The earth also is defiled under the inhabitants thereof; because they have transgressed the laws, changed the ordinance, broken the everlasting covenant. Therefore hath the curse devoured the earth, and they that dwell therein are desolate: therefore the inhabitants of the earth are burned, **and few men left"** (Isaiah 24:1–2, 5–6).

The Bible tells us that during the great deluge "every living substance was destroyed which was upon the face of the ground, both man, and cattle, and the creeping things, and the fowl of the heaven; and they were destroyed from the earth: and **Noah only remained alive**, and they that were with him in the ark" (Genesis 7:23).

After using the sad plight of the wicked of Noah's day as an example, Jesus added, "Watch therefore: for ye know not what hour your Lord doth come" (Matthew 24:42). In other words, do not let the same thing happen to you—do not be the ones taken! Be alert!

Some Will Be "Food For Birds!"

In our last chapter we discussed the prophecy that Jesus made in connection with His second advent, and how, in response to the disciple's question about where the wicked would be "taken," He said unto them that "wheresoever the body is, thither will the eagles be gathered together" (Luke 17:37). The wicked are taken to their destruction.

The fulfillment of this sad prophecy can be found in Revelation 19. There the apostle John elaborates on the tragic events that Jesus mentioned so briefly in Luke 17. In graphic language he portrays the lost as food for the birds, referring to the feast as the "supper of the great God" (Revelation 19:17).

This horrific depiction is preceded by an angelic warning that "Babylon the great is fallen, is fallen, and is become . . . a cage of every unclean and hateful bird. For all nations have drunk of the wine of the wrath of her fornication, and the kings of the earth . . . are waxed rich through the abundance of her delicacies. And I heard another voice from heaven, saying, Come out of her, my people, that ye be not partakers of her sins, and that ye receive not of her plagues" (Revelation 18:2–4).

The revelator follows this indictment with a recital of the judgments pronounced on Babylon, which he calls the "great whore." Then, as Jesus did in Matthew 24 and Luke 17, he turns to the preparation of God's people for the crisis, symbolized by the "marriage supper of the 'Lamb,'" for which His people are dressed in "fine linen, clean and white: for the fine linen is the righteousness of saints" (Revelation 19:8).

Then, the setting of the stage for Christ's return completed, the prophet depicts, in symbolic language, the return of Christ: "And out of his mouth goeth a sharp sword, that with it he should smite the nations: and he shall rule them with a rod of iron: and he treadeth the winepress of the fierceness and wrath of Almighty God. And he hath on his vesture and on his thigh a name written, KING OF KINGS, AND LORD OF LORDS" (Revelation 19:15–16).

As Christ heads toward earth, a strange invitation is given to all the fowls of the air:

"Come and gather yourselves together unto the supper of the great God; that ye may eat the flesh of kings . . . and the flesh of horses, and of them that sit on them, and the flesh of all men, both free and bond, both small and great" (Revelation 19:17–18).

Upon Christ's descent, the opposing army is met, and the fate of the opponents becomes obvious. There is Jesus with a host of shining beings that excel in strength. The prophet states: "And I saw the beast, and the kings of the earth, and their armies, gathered together to make war against him that sat on the horse, and against his army" (Revelation 19:19). Christ's enemies realize their futile and hopeless condition immediately, for John reveals their reaction in an earlier chapter: "The kings of the earth, and the great men, and the rich men, and the chief captains, and the mighty men, and every bondman, and every free man, hid themselves in the dens and in the rocks of the mountains; and said to the mountains and rocks, Fall on us, and hide us from the face of him that sitteth on the throne, and from the wrath of the Lamb: for the great day of his wrath is come and who shall be able to stand?" (Revelation 6:15–17).

As the foiled resistance is put to flight, the leaders of the rebellion are dealt with. "And the beast was **taken** (notice the use of the word 'taken' here again), and with him the false prophet that wrought miracles before him, with which he deceived them that had received the mark of the beast, and them that worshipped his image. These both were cast alive into a lake of fire burning with brimstone" (Revelation 19:20).

Finally, the evil "remnant" (the masses of the wicked) are taken and "slain with the sword" that comes from Christ's mouth (verse 19:21), or, as Paul describes it, "destroy[ed] with the brightness of his coming" (2 Thessalonians 2:8). Then the words of Christ in Luke—depicting death in the context of the bodies and vultures—are fulfilled: "And all the fowls were filled with their flesh" (Revelation 19:21).

Such is the sad fate awaiting the unbelieving and unprepared. It is to avert such a judgment that Jesus gave the warning, not of a secret rapture—but of a judgment that suddenly confronts the uninformed and the ill-prepared.

What irony! We live in an age of advanced knowledge, aware of how tragic the slightest slip of a scalpel can be, or, how devastating a small miscalculation to a major project! We labor tediously over the minutest details to ensure success in our profession. And yet we give little and careless attention to that which is most essential to all humanity—our salvation. Soon Christ shall sweep from the heavens—visible, He assured us, to "every eye" (Revelation 1:7)—to confer immortality upon His faithful remnant. And the supreme irony is that many will be awaiting a secret return, and anticipating at the worst a seven-year period in which they may still repent. Certainly, then, an incorrect understanding of our Lord's return may lead us to deception and even destruction.

God wants us to sit with Him at the banquet table He has prepared for the Great Homecoming rather than be taken to become *food for birds*!

Illustration by Harry Anderson

7

What Should We Do While Waiting?

Honest Activities Are Not Enough—We Have a Work to Do!

From all that we have covered so far, it is safe to conclude that the Second Coming is the greatest cataclysmic event forecasted in all of the Bible. Not only will the coming be supersonically swift, but it will bring about the long predicted and speedy separation between the righteous and the wicked.

In that day all the inhabitants of earth will be caught in one of life's usual pursuits.

Some Will Be Sleeping

The first class affected by the swift separation is described by the "two men in one bed." It is not unusual in many countries for two or more persons to sleep on one bed. I myself grew up sleeping with my brother because my mother, raising us by herself, could afford only three beds for six boys. Addressing this common practice, Jesus spoke of a certain man who was disturbed by a friend at night. The friend came asking for bread to give to his unexpected visitors. But the man responded that he is not able to help because he is in bed, and his children are in bed with him. See Luke 11:5–7.

Apparently, the "two men in one bed" were asleep. They are awakened and separated abruptly—without any time to prepare. Both went to sleep, however, one was ready and the other was not. This same thought is brought out in the parable of the ten virgins (see Matthew 25:1–12). Because of a delay, all the virgins went to sleep. When the bridegroom's party arrives unexpectedly and without any advance warning, the virgins suddenly awaken, but to their dismay the five foolish virgins find themselves caught without ample provisions and an irreversible verdict. The moment of truth had arrived, but it was too late to alter, or reverse their plight.

Some Will Be Working

This same point is made concerning the two women grinding. They are pictured doing their chores, when without warning, their work is abruptly halted. One is snatched away; the other remains. At that moment, neither had any opportunity to plead for more time. One was ready and the other was not. The "two working in a field" were also suddenly stopped from their labor. What had been done or not done, was left that way forever.

Honest Activities Not Enough

There is nothing inherently wrong with any of the activities mentioned in Matthew or Luke. People have always had to plant in order to eat, and today is no exception. Building is an honest occupation and certainly a very necessary trade to meet the demands of the population explosion being experienced today. Marriage was ordained of God, and therefore cannot be considered a sin if conducted after His divine plan and counsel. Eating and drinking are obviously essential for life. Again, if not done to excess, these two activities cannot be considered wrong. So why then did the Lord mention them?

There is a tendency for mankind to become so preoccupied with life's cares and pleasures, that these things can become all-absorbing. The danger exists that, while a person is entrenched in the pursuits of life, the need to prepare for eternity is treated as nonessential.

We can be so everlastingly busy trying to get ahead in life. Our toils and efforts may be beyond reproach and we may be honest about our affairs, yet, there is always the risk that good behavior—even a good moral standing in society—may take the place of the need for spiritual preparedness.

Even a life that is outwardly beyond reproach—like that of Nicodemus (the Jewish religious leader)—can be a formidable barrier to heart preparation. A person may look perfectly good in the eyes of his or her community—yet be devoid of a spiritual life and unworthy of eternal life.

Jesus said, "What shall it profit a man, if he shall gain the whole world, and lose his own soul?" (Mark 8:36). He also cautioned His disciples to "take heed, and beware of covetousness: for a man's life consisteth not in the abundance of the things which he possesseth" (Luke 12:15).

There is nothing that can be taken with us beyond the grave except a godly character. The Pharaohs planned and provided for an abundance of possessions to take into the next life. But today one can view their trophies in museums. While it is true that material goods are important and the proper use of our talents and possessions can demonstrate wise stewardship, they should not be the all-consuming quest of our lives. Our striving for these things should not be at the expense of our eternal salvation.

Placing everything in its proper perspective, Jesus added, "But rather seek ye the kingdom of God; and all these things shall be added unto you" (Luke 12:31). Speaking to a group impressed with His ability to feed thousands, He said, "Labour not for the meat which perisheth, but for that meat which endureth unto everlasting life, which the Son of man shall give unto you: for him hath God the Father sealed" (John 6:27).

Making heaven our first priority places everything else in its proper perspective. Daily taking time to be in a right relationship with our Creator brings the peaceable fruits of righteousness. It also provides opportunity for the development of the kind of character fit for the Kingdom.

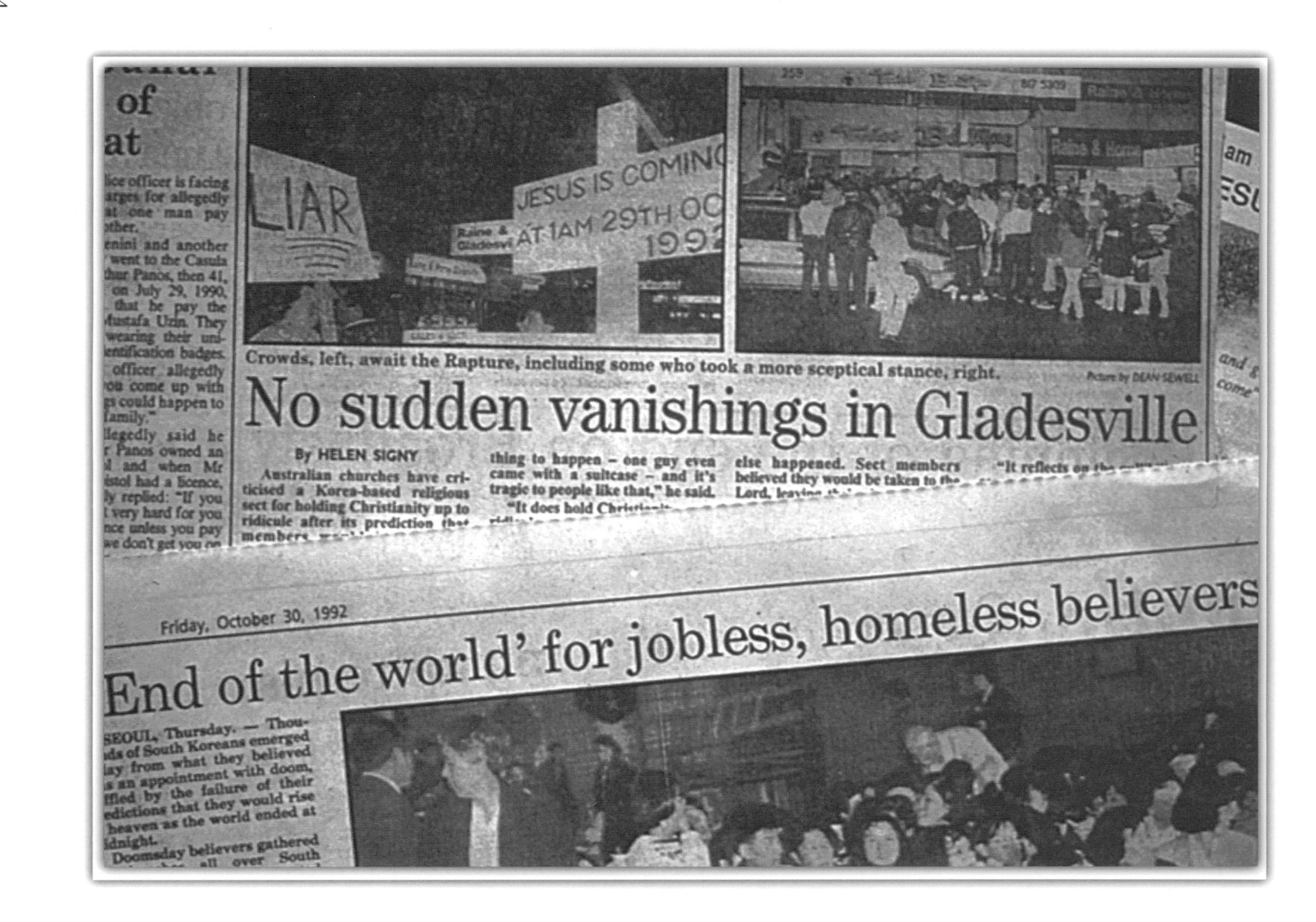

Crowds, left, await the Rapture, including some who took a more sceptical stance, right.

Picture by DEAN SEWELL

No sudden vanishings in Gladesville

By HELEN SIGNY

Australian churches have criticised a Korea-based religious sect for holding Christianity up to ridicule after its prediction that members ...

thing to happen – one guy even came with a suitcase – and it's tragic to people like that," he said.

"It does hold Christi...

else happened. Sect members believed they would be taken to the Lord, leaving ...

"It reflects on the ...

Friday, October 30, 1992

End of the world' for jobless, homeless believers

SEOUL, Thursday. — Thou-...nds of South Koreans emerged ...lay from what they believed ...s an appointment with doom, ...ffled by the failure of their ...edictions that they would rise ...heaven as the world ended at ...idnight.

Doomsday believers gathered ... all over South ...

...ice officer is facing ...arges for allegedly ...at one man pay ...other.

...enini and another ... went to the Casula ...thur Panos, then 41, ... on July 29, 1990, ... that he pay the ...Mustafa Uzin. They ... wearing their uni... ...entification badges. ... officer allegedly ...ou come up with ...s could happen to ...family."

...llegedly said he ...r Panos owned an ...l and when Mr ...istol had a licence, ...ly replied: "If you ...t very hard for you ...nce unless you pay ...we don't get you on ...

8

The Rapture That Wasn't

End of the world, for homeless, jobless believers," and "No sudden vanishings in Gladesville." "The secret rapture declared to occur on October 28, 1992, is the hope they are banking on."

These were the headlines and reports in the Sydney Morning Herald and other Australian newspapers. Many throughout the United States, Korea, as well as other parts of the world, who believed the announcement, embraced the same aspiration. Since it had come from a credible source—their spiritual leaders, the prediction gained more adherents and momentum.

Homes, property, and earthly belongings were abandoned. Through the media it was reported that church leaders among some denominations in Korea obtained legal counsel. They wanted to insure there would be no retraction of the properties donated by their deluded members.

Nevertheless, it was strongly felt by adherents of the doctrine that the predicted occurrence would take place. As far as they were concerned, there was no question, and no doubt. Their hopes would be realized; the event would take place just as foretold. To consider that they would ever again need their homes, lands, or jobs, would to them, be a denial of faith. Sorrow filled some of their hearts, and utter amazement struck others at the incredulous attitude taken by their loved ones, friends, and even some of their own church leaders.

In spite of the ridicule and mockery, believers distributed posters and leaflets far and wide. As excitement continued to increase some even ventured announcements on the radio or other news media. Family radio and other known Christian entities encouraged the frenzy; new adherents were gained as the propaganda was disseminated. There was a general air of jubilance on the part of the believers as the predicted day approached.

The movement also gained momentum in New York City. This is where I first saw the poster attached to a street corner telephone post. As the prediction caught my attention, I decided to follow the unfolding of the events. Knowing the Scriptures as I did, I was very curious to see what would occur on the ominous day.

The "believers" had predicted uncontrolled planes falling out of the skies as their pilots were snatched away. In harmony with their views, Oral

Roberts could vanish before his viewing audience as he made his appeal for more millions. The driverless cars, trucks, trains, and buses left unmanned would certainly create quite a hobbled mess unmatched by any New York traffic jam. Spouses or families would be left in a state of shock by the sudden disappearance of their loved ones. There would be the look of a nameless dread on the faces of those who only half believed, but who now feared the anticipated tribulation to follow.

Of course, the predicted "doomsday" came and went—as uneventful as a rained-out baseball game that never got played. Whatever was to take place never occurred.

A Sad Sequel

It was about ten months later, after the foiled prediction, that I discovered the sequel. I was in Australia when the sad but interesting story unfolded. During my stay in Sydney, I both heard of and met personally some of the people who had actually waited for the event to transpire. They told me how they had stood on the downtown streets of the city to await and experience the fulfillment of the promise on the appointed day. A few were there with suitcases, while others waited with nothing save the clothes they were wearing. All were anxiously expecting the rapturous moment.

But to everyone's disappointment and chagrin, the joyous moment never came; the longed-for swift disappearance never took place!

"Was there a miscalculation?" some wondered, still clinging to their belief. Others felt cheated, deceived, and angry. With hopes dashed in disillusionment, many even became atheists, casting away their beliefs as mere church trickery and lies.

What *Did* Go Wrong?

These unfortunate souls had been "*taken*" by the secret rapture, but not in the way they had expected. They were undoubtedly right about a lot of things, such as the Biblical prediction that:

- Jesus is coming again
- His coming is very soon
- It is important to be ready to meet Him

To their credit, these believers were even willing to make financial sacrifices to help others get ready. Yet, in spite of all the things these believers had right—they were wrong on one very important point: "When" Jesus would come.

It does not matter how much you know about the soon coming of Jesus—if you are wrong about "who" is coming, when He is coming, where He will appear or how He will come, you are likely to be in the wrong place at the wrong time, or, worse yet, looking for the wrong person entirely!

One of the main factors contributing to the people's inability to accept Christ in His first advent was their confused conception concerning the manner of His coming. Their lack of understanding made them ill prepared to receive Him, and as a result they were willing to accept an imposter—Barabbas. Recognizing this fact, it is reasonable to conclude that a misconception concerning the manner of our Lord's second advent will lead the unprepared into accepting an imposter. On the other hand, a proper grasp of what to expect prepares the believer to avoid demonic traps.

An Air of Expectation

There is expectation in the air these days. According to the latest national surveys, the majority of Americans believe that Jesus will come again. It is an expectation that is shared around the world, as increasing numbers of people voice the same feeling. But unfortunately, with this premonition also arises a danger that millions may fall victims to false Christs. In the last two decades, more than one imposter has declared himself to be the Christ. The 1990s episode of the self-proclaimed Christ, David Koresh in Waco, Texas, and its tragic ending, should serve as a warning to us all.

But we need not be deceived. The Word of God offers an abundance of clear statements that will help sincere and diligent seekers arrive at the appropriate understanding. God has given a precious promise that if we "seek the LORD thy God, thou shalt find him, if thou seek him with all thy heart and with all thy soul" (Deuteronomy 4:29).

In the midst of a sea of false ideas and teachings about the rapture, sincere seekers can:

- Know the truth about the Second Coming as taught in God's Holy Word.
- Expose the Myths of the secret rapture.
- Avoid the greatest deception in history, soon to be foisted on the great majority of the world's population.

We can do this, of course, through a careful study of God's Word. There in its holy pages we may learn the "who, when, where, how and why" of Christ's second coming.

The first part of this book gave a Bible-based study of what will happen at the Second Coming of Christ. Now we will expose some of the non-Biblical teachings regarding the secret rapture. Through a careful study of God's Word, we will discover some of the predictions currently being made that, according to the Bible, are simply not going to happen.

9

How the Theory of the Secret Rapture Got Started

Francisco Ribera had a problem on his hands. The dilemma was not his alone, either, for it belonged to the organized church of his day. You see, the Protestant Reformation was making serious inroads into traditional theology. Most notably, they were applying Daniel's prophecies regarding the Antichrist to the medieval church.

Taking exception to the Protestant beliefs, the committed Jesuit priest set out to undermine them with a futuristic, counter reformation tactic of his own.

While many of the Protestant reformers—such as Luther, Calvin, and Knox—taught that the beast of Revelation 13 pointed to the church of the Middle Ages, Ribera taught that the prophecy of the beast and its accompanying mark was neither past nor present, Instead, it would not reveal itself until the "end of the age."

According to Ribera, the Jews would be converted at that time. Then, as the remnant that keeps the commandments of God, the Jewish nation would encounter the beast and the Antichrist and know what the mark of the beast represented. Ribera also taught that Revelation 4 through 18 would be fulfilled in the future, once again at the "end of the age."

Ribera's futuristic teachings soon found their way to England, where they were widely promoted by one Cardinal Bellarmine. John Darby, a Protestant clergyman, who was also a student of the works of Ribera, also accepted and began to propagate Ribera's ideas. In the 1830s one of Darby's parishioners by the name of Margaret McDonald went into a trance and prophesied that Christ could come at any moment and steal away His people. She said that this event would be the beginning of the 'end of the age.' Thus Margaret McDonald, a Protestant, supported Jesuit Ribera's theory.[1]

As for John Darby, he accepted McDonald's vision as a divine endorsement, combined her ideas with Ribera's teaching, and took his amalgamated theory with him to the United States. Although Darby's ideas received a less-than-cordial reception by the main-line denominations of the United States in his day, over time they have crept into and swept through almost every Christian denomination! So much so, in fact, that the idea of a secret rapture is one of the prominent dogmas for a number of churches.

It is amazing that this teaching has become widespread and is believed and preached by so many Protestant ministers—especially in light of the fact that the present teachings of the secret rapture stem from a Jesuit attempt to remove from the medieval church the accusation of Protestant reformers that it was the Antichrist—the beast of Revelation 13. As we have already shown, there are some serious Biblical problems with the teaching of the secret rapture.

Of course, to uncover and solve these problems requires a careful study of texts used to support this popular Christian idea. And in doing so, what better place to begin than with the texts "remembered" by our imaginary character, Evangeline Sincere: "the one shall be taken, and the other left."

[1] Daniel W. O'Fill with Carrol Johnson Shewmake, *What to Say in a Whole New Way,* p. 33. Dave MacPherson, *The Incredible Cover-up,* Omega Publications, pp. 47-77.

Illustration by Lars Justinen

10

Rightly Dividing the Word

Several years ago while "channel surfing" in a Florida motel room, I came across a Sunday morning church service. My attention was arrested, for a popular Florida pastor was speaking on the second coming of Christ. Wondering what he would say on the subject, I decided to listen.

My wife and I were thrilled as he went from text to text, unfolding to his hearers the manner of Christ's coming. Everything seemed to fit together, that is, until he began to refer to the rapture. There the misinformation began. In making his point, the pastor quoted two texts that are commonly used to support the rapture:

- "I tell you, in that night there shall be two men in one bed; the one shall be taken, and the other shall be left. Two women shall be grinding together; the one shall be taken, and the other left. Two men shall be in the field; the one shall be taken, and the other left" (Luke 17:34–36).
- "For the Lord himself shall descend from heaven with a shout, with the voice of the archangel, and with the trump of God: and the dead in Christ shall rise first..." (1 Thessalonians 4:16).

Said the pastor: "The righteous will be snatched away, while the unsaved will be left behind to suffer the tribulation." Notice that in this scenario, common to most versions of the secret rapture, both the righteous and the wicked are left alive.

This position is wrong, and if the Florida pastor had continued on just one more verse in Luke 17, he could have seen it. Notice the context here as we put all three verses together:

> "I tell you, in that night there shall be two men in one bed; the one shall be taken, and the other shall be left. Two women shall be grinding together; the one shall be taken, and the other left. Two men shall be in the field; the one shall be taken, and the other left. And they answered and said unto him, Where, Lord? And he said unto them,

Wheresoever the body is, thither will the eagles be gathered together" (Luke 17:34–37).

Taken Where?

Immediately after Jesus made His statement about one being taken and the other left, the disciples had a question: "Where, Lord?" In other words, they wanted to know "where" the wicked will be taken.

Jesus replied by describing a death scene involving bodies and vultures ("vultures" rather than "eagles" being the better translation).

"And he [Jesus] said unto them, Wheresoever the body is, thither will the eagles be gathered together" (Luke 17:37).

Given the context of this conversation, we can only conclude from Luke 17 that it is not the righteous who are "taken" at all—but the wicked! Those left are the righteous, and they are very much alive. Clearly, when Jesus returns and then leaves, one group is left dead, and one group is left alive. The television preacher was wrong in asserting that both groups live.

As I continued to listen, I could well understand the source of confusion for those dear but deceived people from Sydney, Australia. They were tragically misled by a few misused texts in the Bible. Like the Florida pastor, they ignored a few areas of caution that we should all consider whenever we study the Scriptures.

With this in mind, let us consider and avoid four common "pitfalls" that Christians often fall into when studying God's Word:

Pitfall #1: Wrong Word Usage

One of the challenges in arriving at the proper interpretation of the Scriptures, is *word usage.* This is particularly true with common words such as **take**, **end**, and so forth.

For example, Romans 10:4 says, "For Christ is the end of the law for righteousness to every one that believeth." At first glance, this verse appears to say that Christ finishes or does away with the law. Unfortunately, this is the interpretation most commonly given this verse. This erroneous conclusion is understandable, for this is generally how the word "**end**" is used. However, there are other usages of this word. The adage, "The **end** justifies the means," demonstrates a different application of the word. In this phrase, the use of the word **end** simply means the final outcome.

The Bible also makes use of this meaning. Look at James 5:11. "Behold, we count them happy which endure. Ye have heard of the patience of Job, and have seen the **end** of the Lord; that the Lord is very pitiful, and of tender mercy." Consider also 1 Peter 1:9 which says, "Receiving the **end** of your faith, even the salvation of your souls."

Obviously, if we adhere to the first meaning of the word which most people apply to Romans, we would have to conclude that both the Lord and faith have ended. Since this cannot be true, we are forced to find other definitions for the word. In all of the texts in question, the word ***end*** simply means goal, purpose, or outcome. In other words, the goal of the law is Christ, or the intended purpose of the law is to lead you to Christ.

Pitfall #2: Chronological Flow

Another area which can become a pitfall (and the novice student is not the only one who falls into it), is chronological flow. Some well-meaning Bible researchers fail to take into consideration that not everything written in the Scriptures follows from verse to verse chronologically. A typical example is Revelation 14:14–16, and Revelation, chapter 16. Chapter 14 describes the reaping of the earth, while chapter 16 describes the terrible scourges to come upon the earth before it is harvested.

Pitfall #3: Doctrines Based on One Verse

Coming to a hasty conclusion by making up a doctrine solely on the weight of one or two verses of Scripture is another snare that some fall into. Employing two misused verses of the Bible to make up a teaching can be as disastrous as astronauts missing the moon by just one small degree—the result would be an aimless roaming through space. Or as the Bible puts it, one could be "ever learning, and never able to come to the knowledge of the truth" (2 Timothy 3:7).

The practice of basing an entire doctrine on one verse has contributed to many strange ideas which are still in circulation. It is also a chief cause for the many differing doctrines which have resulted in such a diversity and multiplicity of Christian denominations.

The apostle Paul admonishes us to make sure that we are "rightly dividing the word of truth" (2 Timothy 2:15). One way to achieve this is cross-referencing, or comparing scripture with scripture. Comparing verses will aid us in arriving at a more accurate conclusion, for everything the Bible reveals about one subject is not found in one chapter, or even in one book. That is why the prophet Isaiah wrote, "Precept must be upon precept, precept upon precept; line upon line, line upon line; here a little, and there a little" (Isaiah 28:10).

Pitfall #4: The Power of Suggestion

One other matter which needs to be addressed (though I hasten to add that this by no means is an exhaustive list), is the power of suggestion. Under this power, people are often led to read into scriptures and believe things they have been told are there, when in reality they are not at all.

One of the best illustrations of this is Matthew 5:17. There are many churches teaching today that Jesus was doing away with the obligation of law keeping when He said, "Think not that I am come to destroy the law, or the prophets: I am not come to destroy, but to fulfill." As a result, millions accept this interpretation. However, by putting forth a little effort and examining the context more closely, we may see that the opposite is actually true. For example, the above verse says that Jesus came "not to destroy the law." If He came not to destroy, how can He do away with it? And, if to fulfill means to do away with, then in Matthew 3:15 Jesus must have done away with all righteousness, for He said, "Suffer it to be so now: for thus it becometh us to *fulfill* all righteousness."

Obviously, the idea that Jesus did away with the law cannot be the case. In fact, Jesus revealed His attitude toward and relationship to the law when He said, "He that hath my commandments, and keepeth them, he it is that loveth me: and he that loveth me shall be loved of my Father, and I will love him, and will manifest myself to him. . . . If a man love me, he will keep my words: and my Father will love him, and we will come unto him, and make our abode with him. He that loveth me not keepeth not my sayings: and the word which ye hear is not mine, but the Father's which sent me" (John 14:21, 23–24).

Taking note of the above-mentioned problems may serve in helping to avoid many erroneous conclusions. God has not removed all room for doubt. But He did leave us with the warning, "If any man shall add unto these things, God shall add unto him the plagues that are written in this book: and if any man shall take away from the words of the book of this prophecy, God shall take away his part out of the book of life, and of the holy city, and from the things which are written in this book" (Revelation 22:18–19). This admonition, of itself, serves to undergird the fact that the truth can be arrived at without any additions or deletions from the Word.

A further factor to consider is the difficulty writers have in conveying in a written form all that the eye can see. Writers often cannot in one sweep of the pen express what they have seen. Here is the challenge. We have the ability to see several things happening at the same time. There may be a man on a bike, a woman walking, and a child running. But while with the vision one can register several activities at once, it is quite another matter to record the scene in the same manner as one sees it.

In order for historians to relay what happened in a certain time of earth's history, they have to write it out in layers or tracks. They may first address one aspect, and then go back and cover another. At some point, either by dates or by a statement, they bring it all together, helping the reader to see the full picture of all that transpired in the given period. To get the full picture of what took place when Jesus was on earth, all the information available in the Bible must be gathered. Likewise, in order to see what will happen when Jesus returns, we must gather and arrange all the data pertinent to the subject.

The Bible prophets met with some difficulty when writing out what they saw. Often they themselves did not understand what was revealed to them. For example, Daniel the prophet was given visions that perplexed him. And while at his request he was given some understanding (see Daniel 9:20–22), he was finally told to "shut up the words, and seal the book, even to the time of the end" (Daniel 12:4).

The prophets wrote as they saw. They placed in human language—with all its limitations—divine revelations. Nevertheless, prophets had a deep interest in what was given them to write whether or not they could understand it. The apostle Peter says, "Of which salvation the prophets have inquired and searched diligently, who prophesied of the grace that should come unto you: Searching what, or what manner of time the Spirit of Christ which was in them did signify, when it testified beforehand the sufferings of Christ, and the glory that should follow" (1 Peter 1:10–11). For the seers, to unravel God's mysteries was often an all-absorbing search. And if *they* had to take painstaking efforts, for which they found great rewards, how careful must we be, and how persevering should be our endeavors to achieve our goal of understanding.

11

"The One Shall Be Taken, and the Other Left"

Secret Rapture Teaching: The righteous will be taken, and the wicked left behind for the great tribulation.

What the Bible Says:

"Then shall two be in the field; the one shall be taken, and the other left. Two women shall be grinding at the mill; the one shall be taken, and the other left. Watch therefore: for ye know not what hour your Lord doth come." (Matthew 24:40-42)

This is one of the most popular verses used to support the idea of a secret rapture. According to those who believe in this theory, the verses above refer to the saved or righteous being "taken." The saints are the ones destined for heaven, they argue. As noted earlier, however, the Biblical forerunners of the Second Coming involve the wicked, rather than the righteous, being "taken." For example, those taken to destruction in Noah's day were the wicked, while the righteous were left alive. Of course, defenders of the rapture would be quick to add that the righteous are also "taken"—to heaven. However, this hardly seems to justify reversing the subjects in Matthew 24:40–41—having the saved taken instead of the wicked.

While it is true that only the saved go to heaven, Matthew 24 is focused on the fate of the wicked, rather than on the righteous. Remember the death scene described by Jesus in response to the disciple's inquiry about "where" the wicked would be taken. The idea that Jesus is describing the "taking" of the righteous in Matthew 24:40–41 is simply not consistent with the context of the verses. Jesus is addressing the fate of the unprepared—"Watch therefore," is the warning. Therefore, it must be the wicked, rather than the righteous, who are "taken" to destruction.

Checking the Greek

Some rapturists suggest that the Greek word for "take" in verses 40 and 41 (where Jesus refers to one being left and one taken) of Matthew 24 differs from the word for "take" (translated as "took," where the "flood came and took them all away) in verse 39. This difference, they say, vindicates assuming the righteous are the ones taken in these verses. Let us examine this further:

The Greek word translated "take" in these

verses is *paralambáno*—translated in other texts as "taken" and "taketh." *Paralambáno* refers to taking possession of, as in the story of Joseph taking the child (see Matthew 2:13); taking unto oneself greedily, as in Zacchaeus' case (see Luke 19:8); or taking a hold of, as in the case of Satan taking Jesus up to a high mountain (see Matthew 4:5, 8). Of course, the fact that *paralambáno* may mean "to take unto oneself" does not mean that the outcome is positive. One must consider the context of each verse to determine the result of "taking" or what happens as a consequence of being taken. For example, Satan taking Jesus unto himself to a mountain to tempt Him could certainly not be construed as positive.

Let us consider one more reference that should:

- illustrate the importance of the context, and
- make it crystal clear who is affected by the "taking":

Jesus said, "I tell you, in that night there shall be two men in one bed; the one shall be taken, and the other shall be left. Two women shall be grinding together; the one shall be taken, and the other left. Two men shall be in the field; the one shall be taken, and the other left" (Luke 17:34–36).

The disciples were confused. What was Jesus talking about? Why had He repeated three scenes of abrupt separation? Anxiously, "they answered and said unto him, Where, Lord?" (verse 37). Obviously, the disciples were not asking about the whereabouts of the people who were left behind. Their location is made clear in the context of the verses, where they were described as being either in bed, or grinding, or in the field.

Since we obviously know the location of those who were left behind, it simply would not have been sensible for the disciples to ask where they were. Therefore, the disciple's inquiry must be directed to those "taken."

"What was their destination?" the disciples wanted to know. Jesus replied, "Wherever the dead body is, there will the vultures be gathered together" (Luke 17:37, Amplified Version).

Of course, we know that vultures usually gather where there is something dead. So Jesus' reply can lead to no other conclusion than that the people who are taken are taken to death.

Here at the end of time—just as in Noah's and Lot's day—sudden, tragic death is described as the fate of the unwary. Both in Matthew 24:28 and in Luke 17:37 our Lord used vultures and dead bodies to describe a scenario involving the lost. The question is, Did He use this illustration only as an allegory to teach some lesson, or rather, as a prophetic statement of the events in the future? If prophetic, we should be able to find further Biblical information on the fulfillment.

Look Who is Taken!

As Jesus was teaching His disciples concerning the signs of His advent, He used Matthew 24:36–40 and Luke 17:26–37 to compare the world's condition at the time of the Second Coming—or the time of the end—with two historical events.

As already mentioned, one of these events was the flood in Noah's day; the other was the destruction of Sodom and Gomorrah in Lot's days. Speaking of Noah's day, Jesus said "But as the days of Noe were, so shall also the coming of the Son of man be. For as in the days that were before the flood they were eating and drinking, marrying and giving in marriage, until the day that Noe entered into the ark, and knew not until the flood came, and took them all away; **so shall also the coming of the Son of man be**." (Matthew 24:37–39).

This passage describes the people's attitude in Noah's time, likening it to the prevailing outlook on the part of earth's inhabitants when the Lord appears. It is the activities and attitudes on the part of the lost which will once more call for God's judgments. Concerning Noah's day, we read, "And God saw that the wickedness of man was great in the earth, and that every imagination of the thoughts of his heart was only evil continually. . . . The earth also was corrupt before God, and the earth was filled with violence" (Genesis 6:5, 11).

Looking ahead to this time, the prophet Isaiah wrote, "Fear, and the pit, and the snare, are upon thee, O inhabitant of the earth. And it shall come to pass, that he who fleeth from the noise of the fear shall fall into the pit; and he that cometh up out of the midst of the pit shall be *taken* in the snare: for the windows from on high are open, and the foundations of the earth do shake. The earth is utterly broken down, the earth is clean dissolved, the earth is moved exceedingly. The earth shall reel to and fro like a drunkard, and shall be removed like a cottage; and the transgression thereof shall be heavy upon it; and it shall fall, and not rise again. And it shall come to pass in that day, that the LORD shall punish the host of the high ones that are on high, and the kings of the earth upon the earth" (Isaiah 24:17–21). "Therefore hath the curse devoured the earth, and they that dwell therein are desolate: therefore the inhabitants of the earth are burned, ***and few men left***" (Isaiah 24:6).

In comparison to the billions of people who have lived on planet earth, few will be left. This concept Jesus Himself supported when He said, "Enter ye in at the strait gate: for wide is the gate, and broad is the way, that leadeth to destruction, and many there be which go in thereat: because strait is the gate, and narrow is the way, which leadeth unto life, ***and few there be that find it***" (Matthew 7:13–14).

The apostle Paul writes, "This know also, that in the last days perilous times shall come. For men shall be lovers of their own selves, covetous, boasters, proud, blasphemers, disobedient to parents, unthankful, unholy, without natural affection, trucebreakers, false accusers, incontinent, fierce, despisers of those that are good, traitors, heady, highminded, lovers of pleasures more than lovers of God; having a form of godliness, but denying the power thereof: from such turn away" (2 Timothy 3:1–5).

In Matthew 24 Jesus zeroes in on the analogy of Noah's day and the end of time, even describing the activities of those outside of the ark and their surprising, unfortunate fate. While they were "eating and drinking, marrying and giving in marriage"—busy with the pursuits of life—the end came. After using their sad plight as an example, Jesus then addressed a word of warning to the believers, "Watch therefore: for ye know not what hour your Lord doth come. But know this, that if the goodman of the house had known in what watch the thief would come, he would have watched, and would not have suffered his house to be broken up. Therefore be ye also ready: for in such an hour as ye think not the Son of man cometh" (Matthew 24:42–44). In other words, do not let the same thing happen to you that happened to those outside of the ark—do not be the ones **taken**! Be on the alert!

Illustration by Lars Justinen

12

Deceiving the Very Elect

"If it were possible, they shall deceive the very elect" (Matthew 24:24)

Secret Rapture Teaching

The "very elect" refers to the Jews, who they believe will eventually convert the earth.

What the Bible Says

"For there shall arise false Christs, and false prophets, and shall shew great signs and wonders; insomuch that, if it were possible, they shall deceive the very elect" (Matthew 24:24).

Believers in the secret rapture claim that the Jews, who are supposed to be the "very elect," will convert the people of the earth, and Christ will come to rule it. Hal Lindsey, *The Late Great Planet Earth*, pp. 54, 111, 143. However, Christ did not commit the final preaching of the gospel to Israel as a nation. Although the disciples were physical Jews, and responded to the call to herald the gospel message, their election to preach the gospel was not based solely on race. Neither was the preaching of the gospel limited to them exclusively. It is interesting to note that the mighty preaching of the gospel in the early Christian church was accomplished by a cosmopolitan group of believers. Even on the day of Pentecost, when the Spirit was poured out in power, it resulted in a gathering of new converts who were composed of "Jews and proselytes." (Acts 2:10). The early rain power brought together true-hearted converts of Jews and Gentiles alike who in turn went out to preach.

This same election will happen when the latter rain occurs. The Spirit of God will be poured out on all flesh. The prophet Joel predicts: "And it shall come to pass afterward, that I will pour out my spirit upon all flesh; and your sons and your daughters shall prophesy, your old men shall dream dreams, your young men shall see visions: and also upon the servants and upon the handmaids in those days will I pour out my spirit. And I will shew wonders in the heavens and in the earth, blood, and fire, and pillars of smoke. The sun shall be turned into darkness, and the moon into blood, before the great and the terrible day of the LORD come. And it shall come to pass, that whosoever shall call on the name of the LORD shall be delivered: for in mount Zion and in Jerusalem shall be deliverance, as the LORD hath said, and in the remnant whom the LORD shall call" (Joel 2:28-32). Both Gentiles and Jews will take up the proclamation of the gospel with power, and the earth will be lightened with His glory!

Speaking to His disciples and to all followers in future generations, Jesus said, "Go ye therefore, and teach all nations, baptizing them in the name of the Father, and of the Son, and of the Holy Ghost: teaching them to observe all things whatsoever I have commanded you: and, lo, I am with you alway, even unto the end of the world" (Matthew 28:19–20). And in the book of Mark He is recorded as saying: "Go ye into all the world, and preach the gospel to every creature. He that believeth and is baptized shall be saved; but he that believeth not shall be damned" (Mark 16:15–16).

The "go ye" commission is general. It is not limited to a race or a nation. It is given to all believers. Jesus said, "And the Spirit and the bride say, Come. And let him that heareth say, Come. And let him that is athirst come. And whosoever will, let him take the water of life freely" (Revelation 22:17). When this gospel is preached by the converted believers to all the world, then will the end come. This, Jesus made clear when he stated, "And this gospel of the kingdom shall be preached in all the world for a witness unto all nations; and then shall the end come" (Matthew 24:14).

It is those who believe in Him who are called the "elect." They comprise the final true Israel. This "elect body of believers" will be made up of converted physical Jews as well as converted Gentiles. At the coming of Christ, the word "elect" is given in reference to all who will be saved. Jesus declares, "And he shall send his angels with a great sound of a trumpet, and they shall gather together his ***elect*** from the four winds, from one end of heaven to the other" (Matthew 24:31). The Apostle Paul uses this title to include all believers. He writes, "What shall we then say to these things? If God be for us, who can be against us? He that spared not his own Son, but delivered him up for us all, how shall he not with him also freely give us all things? Who shall lay any thing to the charge of God's ***elect***? It is God that justifieth." (Romans 8:31-33). Peter himself had the same understanding. He used the term to include all believers. Writing to those scattered about, he wrote: "Peter, an apostle of Jesus Christ, to the strangers scattered throughout Pontus, Galatia, Cappadocia, Asia, and Bithynia, **elect** according to the foreknowledge of God the Father, through sanctification of the Spirit, unto obedience and sprinkling of the blood of Jesus Christ: Grace unto you, and peace, be multiplied" (1 Peter 1:1–2).

The question then arises, Who is a true Jew? Speaking of this, Paul says, "For he is not a Jew, which is one outwardly; neither is that circumcision, which is outward in the flesh: but he is a Jew, which is one inwardly; and circumcision is that of the heart, in the spirit, and not in the letter; whose praise is not of men, but of God" (Romans 2:28–29). Continuing in the same vein, he said, "For they are not all Israel, which are of Israel: Neither, because they are the seed of Abraham, are they all children: but, In Isaac shall thy seed be called.

That is, They which are the children of the flesh, these are not the children of God: but the children of the promise are counted for the seed" (Romans 9:6–8). For, "They which are of faith, the same are the children of Abraham. . . . For as many of you as have been baptized into Christ have put on Christ. There is neither Jew nor Greek . . . there is neither male nor female: for ye are all one in Christ Jesus. And if ye be Christ's, then are ye Abraham's seed, and heirs according to the promise" (Galatians 3:7, 27–29). In the book of Romans, he says, "What then? Israel hath not obtained that which he seeketh for; but the **election** hath obtained it, and the rest were blinded" (Romans 11:7). That physical Jews will have a part in the final heralding of the gospel is clear in the scripture. Paul writes: "And they also, if they abide not still in unbelief, shall be grafted in: for God is able to graft them in again. For if thou [speaking of Gentiles] wert cut out of the olive tree which is wild by nature, and wert grafted contrary to nature into a good olive tree: how much more shall these, which be the natural *branches*, be grafted into their own olive tree?" (Romans 11:23–24).

From the light given us in these passages, it is clear that it is not physical Israel as a nation that is to "preach the gospel and then shall the end come." Rather, it will be spiritual Israel, made up of Jews and Gentiles. They are those who, like Jacob of old, wrestle with God, gain the victory over sin, and are incorporated under the name Israelites. These are the elect of God who "overcame . . . by the blood of the Lamb, and by the word of their testimony; and loved not their lives unto the death." These are the true Jews. If you accept Jesus as your Saviour, you too become a spiritual Jew, an heir to the promises of your spiritual father Abraham. By accepting Christ you are grafted into the root (see Romans, chapter 11).

The attempt to place the application to a physical, literal Israel serves as a good decoy. It provides for a perfect distraction from the plot. And while the elect are distracted, looking for the fulfillment to occur elsewhere with other people, it robs them of the true privileges they have. And if the elect are others and not themselves, then it can tend to take away from their vigilance. The warning is for all that claim to be true believers in Jesus, and who by His grace become the elect.

The warning concerning false Christs is for us.

13

We Shall All Be Changed

"We shall all be changed, in a moment, in the twinkling of an eye" (1 Corinthians 15:51-52)

Secret Rapture Teaching

The saints will "mysteriously disappear" at the time of the secret rapture.

What the Bible Says

> *"Behold, I shew you a mystery; we shall not all sleep, but we shall all be changed, in a moment, in the twinkling of an eye, at the last trump: for the trumpet shall sound, and the dead shall be raised incorruptible, and we shall be changed"* (1 Corinthians 15:51–52).

This verse is used to explain the supposed mysterious disappearance that is to occur when the saved are snatched up. Referring to the seven trumpets of Revelation, those who believe in the rapture teach that the mysterious "snatching" takes place first, then each trumpet will give its blast during the seven years of tribulation in equal intervals.

However, right there in verse 52 it says that the transformation takes place *at the last trump—not* ***before*** *the last trump.* In addition, our Lord connects the sounding of the trumpet with His second coming and the gathering of the saints. Jesus said, "And he shall send his angels with a great sound of a trumpet, and they shall gather together his elect from the four winds, from one end of heaven to the other" (Matthew 24:31).

Both references place the gathering of God's people after the trumpet sounds—not before. In fact, concerning the tribulation, Jesus not only places His own appearance after it, but the sounding of the trumpet as well. The record states, "Immediately after the tribulation of those days shall the sun be darkened, and the moon shall not give her light, and the stars shall fall from heaven, and the powers of the heavens shall be shaken: and then shall appear the sign of the Son of man in heaven: and then shall all the tribes of the earth mourn, and they shall see the Son of man coming in the clouds of heaven with power and great glory" (Matthew 24:29–30).

There was no doubt in the apostle's mind

concerning the sequence of the chain of events. Once again he makes his poignant point to the Thessalonians: "For this we say unto you by the word of the Lord, that we which are alive and remain unto the coming of the Lord shall not prevent them which are asleep. For the Lord himself shall descend from heaven with a shout, with the voice of the archangel, and with the trump of God: and the dead in Christ shall rise first: then we which are alive and remain shall be caught up together with them in the clouds, to meet the Lord in the air: and so shall we ever be with the Lord" (1 Thessalonians 4:15–17). As always, the trump of God precedes the translation of the saints who remain alive to see His glorious appearance and to hear the blasts of the heavenly trumpeters.

Illustration by Lars Justinen

14

Confirming the Covenant

"And he shall confirm the covenant with many for one week: and in the midst of the week he shall cause the sacrifice and the oblation to cease."

Secret Rapture Teaching

The seven-year period spoken of by Daniel predicts a "great tribulation," and is still in the future.

What the Bible Says

"Seventy weeks are determined upon thy people and upon thy holy city, to finish the transgression, and to make an end of sins, and to make reconciliation for iniquity, and to bring in everlasting righteousness, and to seal up the vision and prophecy, and to anoint the most Holy. Know therefore and understand, that from the going forth of the commandment to restore and to build Jerusalem unto the Messiah the Prince shall be seven weeks, and threescore and two weeks: the street shall be built again, and the wall, even in troublous times. And after threescore and two weeks shall Messiah be cut off, but not for himself: and the people of the prince that shall come shall destroy the city and the sanctuary; and the end thereof shall be with a flood, and unto the end of the war desolations are determined. And he shall confirm the covenant with many for one week: and in the midst of the week he shall cause the sacrifice and the oblation to cease" (Daniel 9:24–27).

Those who believe in the secret rapture, in following the teachings of Francisco Ribera, teach that the seven-year period spoken of by the prophet Daniel is still in the future. However, a careful study of Daniel reveals that the seven-year period has nothing to do with a "great tribulation." Rather, it was a prophecy that was fulfilled in the time of Christ!

This prediction is part of the twenty-three-hundred-day prophecy of Daniel 8:14, which reveals that the sanctuary would be cleansed at the end of the predicted time. But in order for

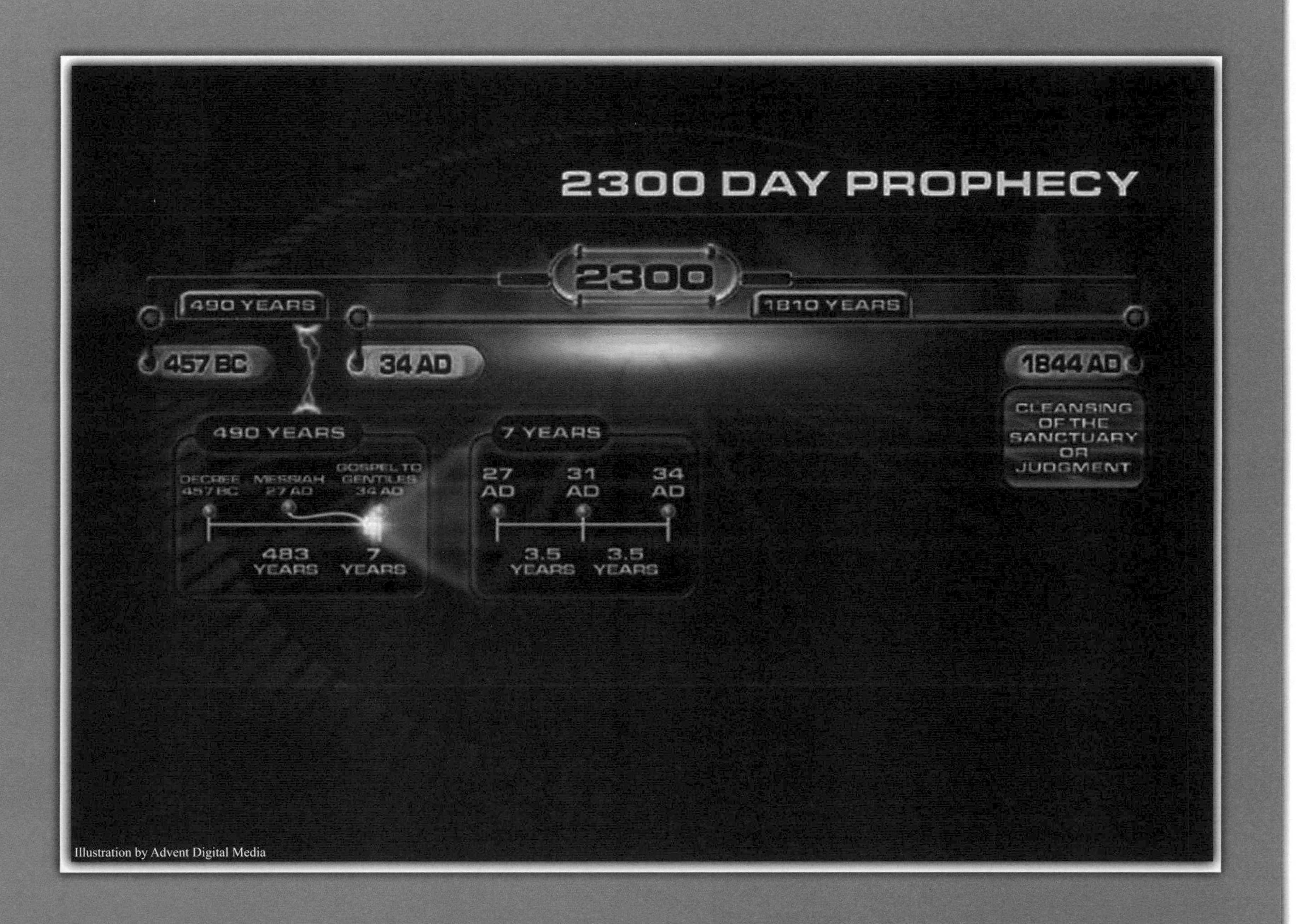

Illustration by Advent Digital Media

that to take place, several other things had to transpire first. Jerusalem and the sanctuary must be rebuilt. After the reconstruction, the sacrifices would cease as a result of the Messiah's coming and being cut off, making an atonement with His own blood on behalf of God's people. This particular part of the prophecy (see Daniel 9:24–27) was actually given to pinpoint when the Messiah would come, what He would do, and, finally, when He would die. All this was fulfilled two thousand years ago.

Let us now consider the prophecy part by part. We begin with the introduction:

"Seventy weeks are determined upon thy people."

Daniel was a Jew. He and his people were in captivity in Babylon, and it is to them that this message was given. The 70 weeks is a prophetic period of 490 years. Why is it years? Because, the Scriptures tells us that a prophetic day represents a year. Numbers 14:34 sheds light on this: "After the number of the days in which ye searched the land, even forty days, each day for a year . . . even forty years." So God established the principle that one day equals a year. This concept is also supported by the prophet Ezekiel: "I have appointed thee each day for a year" (Ezekiel 4:6).

Now that we have the key, let us apply it to determine the starting point. The angel said, "Know therefore and understand, that from the going forth of the commandment to restore and to build Jerusalem unto the Messiah the Prince shall be seven weeks, and threescore and two weeks [or 69 weeks]" (Daniel 9:25). The time clock would start ticking when the command to start the building of Jerusalem would be issued. According to history, and also in the book of Ezra, chapters 7 and 8, a decree by Artaxerxes to restore Jerusalem was given and finally executed about the middle of the year 457 B.C. Thus, the 490 years would start in 457 B.C.

From that starting point, verse 25 says that 69 of the 70 weeks brings us to the Messiah. The 69 weeks are 483 years which would start in 457 B.C. and end in A.D. 27. Once the Messiah appeared, there would remain one week. Then in the midst of the week, or at the conclusion of three-and-one-half years, the Messiah would be "cut off, but not for himself" (verse 27). As a result of being "cut off," the covenant would be confirmed causing the sacrifices to cease. After this, there would yet remain three-and-one-half years bringing the prophecy to its completion in A.D. 34.

Amazing Fulfillments

It is amazing that in these passages the Bible is revealing precisely when Jesus would begin His ministry as the Messiah, and when He would give His life as the Lamb of God. Now the question is, Did our Lord and Saviour begin His ministry and was He also anointed in A.D. 27? Let us see what the Bible says: "Now in the fifteenth year of the reign of Tiberius Caesar, Pontius Pilate being governor of Judaea, and Herod being tetrarch of Galilee, and his brother Philip tetrarch of Ituraea and of the region of Trachonitis, and Lysanias the tetrarch of Abilene, Annas and Caiaphas being the high priests, the word of God came unto John the son of Zacharias in the wilderness. And he came into all the country about Jordan, preaching the baptism of repentance for the remission of sins" (Luke 3:1–3). Now notice that Tiberius Caesar began to rule in A.D. 12. In the fifteenth year of his reign, Pontius Pilate began his governorship. This brings us to A.D. 27.

Not only did Jesus start His ministry in that year, but He was also anointed the same year. It was precisely in this year that John the Baptist began to preach and to baptize. The record states: "And it came to pass in those days, that Jesus came from Nazareth of Galilee, and was baptized of John in Jordan. And straightway coming up out of the water, he saw the heavens opened, and the Spirit like a dove descending upon him: and there came a voice from heaven, saying, Thou art my beloved Son, in whom I am well pleased" (Mark 1:9–11).

Concerning this event, Paul said, "God anointed Jesus of Nazareth with the Holy Spirit and power" (Acts 10:38, NIV). Isn't it remarkable that John was baptizing exactly in the year God had foretold that the Messiah would be anointed? Indeed, then, our Saviour was anointed and began His ministry in A.D. 27.

Jesus concluded His ministry three-and-one-half years later. He was crucified for you and for me. And when He died, He caused "the sacrifice and oblation to cease." Referring to the hour of His final agony, when our Lord breathed His last breath, John writes, "Jesus, when he had cried again with a loud voice, yielded up the ghost. And, behold, the veil of the temple was rent in twain from the top to the bottom; and the earth did quake, and the rocks rent" (Matthew 27:50–51). This veil of the temple was a curtain approximately 70 feet high that separated the holy place from the Most Holy Place. When Jesus died, an unseen hand tore the curtain from top to bottom, showing that God's presence would no longer be there, and that there would be no more a need to offer animal sacrifices. Why?—Because Jesus, the real Lamb, took the place of the substitute. His death paid the penalty in full for your sins and mine. As the Bible had said, the sacrifices did cease on that day and have never resumed since.

One day while visiting in New York City, I took a subway train ride. Looking for a seat, I spotted an empty one next to a Hasidic (an orthodox) Jew. It was not long before we entered into a conversation. "Tell me something," I said, "when did the sacrificing of lambs come to an end?" "Well," he said, "to be honest, it was sometime around the time of Christ." It was interesting for a Hasidic Jew to tell me that! Yes, our Master did die; he did pay the penalty for sin. He bore your sins and mine, and thus by his death he swept away the system of sacrifices forever.

After His three-and-one-half years of ministry came to an end, there remained three-and-one-half years more to complete the seventy-week prophecy. The additional time brings us to the year A.D. 34. What was to happen? Even after the people of God had cried out, "Crucify him, crucify him!" God still gave His people three-and-one-half years more. Oh, the love of God! How great is His patience! How He longs to save us! How willing He is to receive us! He is "not willing that any should perish, but that all should come to repentance" (2 Peter 3:9). Think of it: three-and-one-half years more after they had crucified His beloved Son!

The question is, Did they respond? According to Scriptures, most of them did not. The time of added probation did not profit the nation. By the stoning of Stephen, and the persecuting of the first disciples, they brought their grace period to an end in A.D. 34.

Luke writes, "And Saul was consenting unto his death. And at that time there was a great persecution against the church which was at Jerusalem; and they were all scattered abroad throughout the regions of Judaea and Samaria, except the apostles. . . . Therefore they that were scattered abroad went every where preaching the word" (Acts 8:1, 4). God turned the gospel to the Gentiles; and today the Gentiles are preaching the everlasting gospel through the habitable globe. This brings the seventy-week prophecy to an end.

When one considers that Daniel's 70-week prophecy was given for the specific purpose of making the identity of the true Christ unequivocally clear, so that nobody but Jesus Himself could in any way, shape, or form have so accurately fulfilled all the details and specifications of this great time prediction, one can only marvel. Taken in this light, it is mind-boggling to think that anyone could dare to take part of this great Messianic prophecy and swing it into the far distant future by applying it to some supposed seven-year tribulation and the Antichrist. What a travesty!

15

Those Which Sleep in Jesus

"So them also which sleep in Jesus will God bring with Him."

Secret Rapture Teaching

At the second coming of Christ "after the great tribulation", God will bring the "saints" who have already gone to heaven with Him.

What the Bible Says

"But I would not have you to be ignorant, brethren, concerning them which are asleep, that ye sorrow not, even as others which have no hope. For if we believe that Jesus died and rose again, even so them also which sleep in Jesus will God bring with him" (1 Thessalonians 4:13–14).

Those who believe in a secret rapture use this text to show that when Christ comes He will bring the saints who have already died and risen to heaven with Him. In studying this out, let us look at some newer Bible versions to help clarify the meaning of this text:

"So also will God bring forth with him them who have fallen asleep through Jesus." Rhm. Version, *The Emphasized New Testament: A New Translation* (J. B. Rotheham).

Another translation puts it this way; "So also will God, through Jesus, bring back those who sleep, together with Him." *Conversion, The Epistles of Paul*, (W. J. Conybeare).

In other words, those who have died in the faith of Jesus, and who are still here on the earth when Jesus comes, will be gathered and carried away by Him to heaven. The Greek phrase for "bring with Him" is αξε συν αυτω. Αξει is the future tense of αγω. One of the meanings of αγω in Liddell and Scott, is "carry away captive." The cross-reference of this verse is Ephesians 4:8: "Wherefore he saith, When he ascended up on high, he led captivity captive, and gave gifts unto men." While Paul uses a different verb in this verse, it carries the same idea. The phrase had a special military meaning—to rescue prisoners of war. Therefore, Jesus is coming to rescue those who have been in the prison house of the graves.

Even though textual evidence clearly shows that it is speaking about those who "sleep in Jesus" at the time of His coming, those who believe in a secret rapture have them awake and returning with Jesus instead. These are those (they say), who from a previous disappearance, or who died earlier, were taken to heaven, and at His coming are brought back from heaven to earth with Christ.

Obviously, if they are asleep (or dead), they must first be awakened or resurrected before the Lord can do anything with them. Paul himself did not teach that he or the Christians would come back with Jesus. Rather, he expected to be gathered unto the Lord at His coming. He warns, "Now we beseech you, brethren, by the coming of our Lord Jesus Christ, **and by our gathering together unto him**, that ye be not soon shaken in mind, or be troubled, neither by spirit, nor by word, nor by letter as from us, as that the day of Christ is at hand" (2 Thessalonians 2:1–2).

Jesus Himself did not teach that He would bring saints with Him. Instead, His words give evidence that the dead remaining on earth necessitated His return. "And this is the Father's will which hath sent me, that of all which he hath given me I should lose nothing, but should raise it up again at the last day. And this is the will of him that sent me, that every one which seeth the Son, and believeth on him, may have everlasting life: and I will raise him up at the last day. . . . No man can come to me, except the Father which hath sent me draw him: and I will raise him up at the last day. . . . Whoso eateth my flesh, and drinketh my blood, hath eternal life; and I will raise him up at the last day" (John 6:39–40, 44, 54).

Four times Jesus repeated the phrase, "at the last day." Though the believers are promised eternal life as soon as they believe, they do not experience it until they are raised up in the last day. This last day is equated with the day of judgment. Of this Jesus said, "He that rejecteth me, and receiveth not my words, hath one that judgeth him: the word that I have spoken, the same shall judge him in the last day" (John 12:48).

When Lazarus, the friend of Jesus, was struck with death, Jesus went to resurrect him. Upon meeting the Lord, Martha, the dead man's sister, said to Him, "if thou hadst been here, my brother had not died" (John 11:21). To which Jesus responded, "Thy brother shall rise again" (John 11:23).

"I know that he shall rise again in the resurrection at the last day," Martha replied (John 11:24). This truth was the hope that Martha held onto. However, she did not understand that the One who had power to raise the dead in the last day was right there in her presence. And true to His word, the dead Lazarus did rise. This gave those believers, as it should also give us, the assurance of Christ's power to raise the sleeping saints when He returns in glory at the last day.

16

As a Thief in the Night

"But the day of the Lord will come as a thief in the night…"

Secret Rapture Teaching

The coming of Jesus will be swift and in secret.

What the Bible Says

> *"But the day of the Lord will come as a thief in the night; in the which the heavens shall pass away with a great noise, and the elements shall melt with fervent heat, the earth also and the works that are therein shall be burned up"* (2 Peter 3:10).

Those who believe in the rapture, tie this text in with the swift and secret appearance of Christ. But have you ever been the victim of a thief? If you have, then you understand perfectly well the reason why Peter, Paul, and our Lord employ this analogy.

Speaking to His disciples, Jesus said, "Sell that ye have, and give alms; provide yourselves bags which wax not old, a treasure in the heavens that faileth not, where no **thief** approacheth, neither moth corrupteth. For where your treasure is, there will your heart be also. Let your loins be girded about, and your lights burning; and ye yourselves like unto men that wait for their lord, when he will return from the wedding; that when he cometh and knocketh, they may open unto him immediately. Blessed are those servants, whom the lord when he cometh shall find watching: verily I say unto you, that he shall gird himself, and make them to sit down to meat, and will come forth and serve them. And if he shall come in the second watch, or come in the third watch, and find them so, blessed are those servants. And this know, that if the goodman of the house had known what hour the **thief** would come, he would have watched, and not have suffered his house to be broken through. Be ye therefore ready also: for the Son of man cometh at an hour when ye think not" (Luke 12:33–40).

A thief approaches the scene of the crime stealthily, and unobserved. Unfortunately for the ill-fated person, the thief's presence usually is discovered after the fact. Though his immediate appearance seems like that of a phantom who appears and disappears, he is not invisible. His arrival, though tangible and very physical, is always unannounced and unexpected—he comes when you least expect him.

In another verse of scripture, Jesus said, "Behold, I come as a **thief.** Blessed is he that watcheth, and keepeth his garments, lest he walk naked, and they see his shame" (Revelation 16:15.) Again, He said, "Remember therefore how thou hast received and heard, and hold fast, and repent. If therefore thou shalt not watch, I will come on thee as a **thief,** and thou shalt not know what hour I will come upon thee" (Revelation 3:3). The Lord does not use this example to portray His own character; for He is holy, just, and good. Neither does He employ it to hint that His coming is of an invisible nature as some teach, but rather that just as the thief uses an element of surprise, so His coming will be of the same nature.

Emphasizing this fact the apostle Paul writes, "For yourselves know perfectly that the day of the Lord so cometh as a **thief** in the night" (1 Thessalonians 5:2). Along with the day of the Lord coming as a thief in the night, Paul links a sudden destruction which is to result from the Lord's coming. He writes, "For when they shall say, Peace and safety; then sudden destruction cometh upon them, as travail upon a woman with child; and they shall not escape" (1 Thessalonians 5:3).

The disciple Peter also contributes to this combination of the coming as a thief with destruction. Considering 2 Peter 3:10, again we read, "But the day of the Lord will come as a **thief** in the night; in the which the heavens shall pass away with a great noise, and the elements shall melt with fervent heat, the earth also and the works that are therein shall be burned up."

It was this element of surprise and its accompanying devastation that caught the people off guard in Noah's day. The unanticipated flood came. Those unbelieving antediluvians were caught by that incredible, unsuspecting deluge. Like a thief, that terrible destruction came with relentless force upon that wicked generation. And contrary to the notion that the coming of Christ will be invisible, Jesus' own words, "as in the days of Noe, so shall also the coming of the Son of man be," make it obvious that His coming will be just as visible, tangible, and devastating as the waters that flooded the earth.

No doubt, the results of Jesus' coming will surpass in magnitude the flood, and the destruction of Sodom and Gomorrah. Everything on earth shall be affected. Just as Noah and the people of his day experienced the flood, so will the righteous and the wicked also experience that momentous event when it comes.

However, there will be one major difference with our Lord's coming: Unlike the days after Noah and Lot's time, which allowed sin to take root again and contaminate the earth, the return of Jesus at the Second Coming will make everything final.

Admonishing us concerning the stealthy appearance of our Lord, and the irrevocable consequences of this event, Saint Peter writes, "Seeing then that all these things shall be dissolved, what manner of persons ought ye to be in all holy conversation and godliness, looking for and hasting unto the coming of the day of God, wherein the heavens being on fire shall be dissolved, and the elements shall melt with fervent heat? Nevertheless we, according to his promise, look for new heavens and a new earth, wherein dwelleth righteousness. Wherefore, beloved, seeing that ye look for such things, be diligent that ye may be found of him in peace, without spot, and blameless" (2 Peter 3:11–14).

17

The Man of Sin Revealed

"That day shall not come, except there come a falling away first, and that man of sin be revealed, the son of perdition; who opposeth and exalteth himself above all that is called God, or that is worshipped; so that he as God sitteth in the temple of God, shewing himself that he is God…"

Secret Rapture Teaching

The Antichrist will be a Roman dictator, who will sit in a temple rebuilt in Jerusalem," and that he will rule the world for three and a half years.

What the Bible Says

"Now we beseech you, brethren, by the coming of our Lord Jesus Christ, and by our gathering together unto him, that ye be not soon shaken in mind, or be troubled, neither by spirit, nor by word, nor by letter as from us, as that the day of Christ is at hand. Let no man deceive you by any means: for that day shall not come, except there come a falling away first, and that man of sin be revealed, the son of perdition; who opposeth and exalteth himself above all that is called God, or that is worshipped; so that he as God sitteth in the temple of God, shewing himself that he is God" (2 Thessalonians 2:1–4).

Believers in the rapture use the above text to support the idea that "the Antichrist will be a Roman dictator, who will sit in a temple rebuilt in Jerusalem," and that he will rule the world for three and a half years. Hal Lindsey, *The Rapture*, Bantam books, p. 128.

In analyzing these claims, let us first look more closely at the word *temple*. The Greek word for temple is "ναωσ." In *Young's Analytical Concordance* this word is found in at least forty different references, and refers in a spiritual sense to a "dwelling place."

Thus in Paul's writings, the temple of God, or the ναωσ, is the church—not some future temple to be built in Jerusalem by unbelieving Jews. Using this word, Paul says, "Know ye not that *ye* are the **temple** of God and that the Spirit of God dwelleth in you? If any man defile the **temple** of God, him shall God destroy; for the **temple** of God is holy, which **temple** *ye* are" (1 Corinthians 3:16–17).

Paul did not see a future temple being built, for he well knew that the earthly temple had given way to the heavenly. See Hebrews, chapters 8 and 9. That he saw the temple as the church of God is further made clear by the following texts: "What agreement hath the temple of God with idols? for [*WE*] are the temple of the living God" (2 Corinthians 6:16, R.V). And again to the Ephesians he wrote: "[Ye] are built upon the foundation of the apostles and prophets, Jesus Christ himself being the chief corner stone; in whom all the building fitly framed together groweth unto an holy **temple** in the Lord; in whom **ye** *also* are builded together for an habitation of God through the Spirit" (Ephesians 2:20–22).

Therefore, the temple of God is not some edifice to be erected in Jerusalem and occupied by a world dictator, but it is comprised of people. In fact, an entirely different Greek word, "Ηιερον," is utilized when the Bible refers to the literal temple.

In contrast, the word "ναωσ" is used to refer to the spiritual temple. For example, in the book of Revelation (which uses the word "ναωσ" 16 times), Jesus promises that those who overcome "will I make a pillar in the **temple** (ναωσ) of my God" (Revelation 3:12).

This obviously could not be in a literal sense, for a man could not be a physical pillar. The language used must be figurative or have a spiritual significance.

As already stated, it is said that this Antichrist is a "Roman dictator." Nevertheless, the word Antichrist does not express this idea at all. The word is made up of two Greek words; Anti and Christ. The word Anti does not mean against, as it is used today, but rather "instead of," "in the room of," or "substitution." *Strong's Analytical Concordance*. The word Christ was derived from the Hebrew word Messiah, which means, the "Anointed One." Putting the two definitions together, we arrive at the meaning—**in the place of the ordained One**, or the **substitute for God's Holy One**.

It is because of the difficulty of unmasking this villain, who masquerades himself and his acts in the place of Christ, that the Bible gives the warning. The "man of sin be revealed, the son of perdition; who opposeth and exalteth himself above all that is called God, or that is worshipped; so that he as God sitteth in the temple of God, shewing himself that he is God." (2 Thessalonians 2:3–4).

From this verse we see that the Antichrist must seek to usurp Christ's place. Of course, in order to pull off this overmastering delusion, he must be able to imitate the Saviour; or have a likeness to Him by showing Christlike attributes. This he must accomplish by replacing those things which definitely identify the true Lord as Creator and Redeemer, and substituting them with those teachings or acts which direct the attention of the people to him rather than to Jesus.

Speaking of the "man of sin" the text refers to him as "the son of perdition." There is only one person in the whole of scriptures given that name. That person is Judas. Speaking of him, Jesus said, "While I was with them in the world . . . none of them is lost, but the son of perdition; that the scripture might be fulfilled" (John 17:12). He was the disciple of Christ who betrayed and sold Jesus for thirty pieces of silver. Judas began as a disciple and ended as an apostate.

It follows, therefore, that if we are going to look for the man of sin, we should begin by looking not for a hardened dictator who is ruthless and rules by force, but rather by looking for an apostate, a betrayer from within the church. As Judas sold his Lord, so this leader and his system must sell out Christ and His truth. There must be an attempt to substitute Christ by utilizing His ways, and even His own teachings. The deception must come not from paganism, or atheism, but from where people least expect it—from within professed Christianity. The Antichrist therefore must be able to lead people to give their loyalties to him who so artfully parades himself as Christ. The deception must be so cunning that it takes not only the lost multitudes, but also, if possible, the very elect.

18

Signs

And there shall be signs in the sun, and in the moon, and in the stars; and upon the earth distress of nations, with perplexity; the sea and the waves roaring; men's hearts failing them for fear, and for looking after those things which are coming on the earth: for the powers of heaven shall be shaken."

Secret Rapture Teaching

There will be a stupendous time of trouble, known as the "great tribulation", at the end of the world.

What the Bible Says

"And there shall be signs in the sun, and in the moon, and in the stars; and upon the earth distress of nations, with perplexity; the sea and the waves roaring; men's hearts failing them for fear, and for looking after those things which are coming on the earth: for the powers of heaven shall be shaken" (Luke 21:25–26).

Believers in a secret rapture point to the above text, among others as giving the details of the "Great Tribulation" they expect to occur after the secret rapture has taken place. After the expected disappearance of the saints, the world is to be hurled into a stupendous time of trouble. According to them, only those who have been fortunate enough to be snatched away will escape the agony.

Popular portrayals of the suffering to be experienced during this time are enough to make anyone tremble. No wonder people are anxious to accept some foolproof escape. In fact, if I accepted the horror portrayed in this doctrine, I, too, would probably be looking for such a fantastic escape route.

Our Lord did predict that trouble would increase, and His prediction has come true. While earthquakes have become more numerous and greater in power, there has also been an increase in disasters by land, air and sea as storms increase in their destructive force. In fact, hurricanes that at one time would have been classed as third category hurricanes (with winds of up to 75 miles per hour) are now considered fifth category hurricanes. The new third category hurricane covers those with winds of up to 200 miles per hour, as in the case of Hurricane Andrew.

Some scientists attribute this increase in natural disasters to the "warming affect," and to our modern-day ability to destroy the earth. Relative to these phenomena, Jesus said, "And the nations were angry, and thy wrath is come, and the time of the dead, that they should be judged, and that thou shouldest give reward unto thy servants the prophets, and to the saints, and them that fear thy name, small and great; and shouldest destroy them which destroy the earth" (Revelation 11:18).

Pestilences will mount up and plague whole populaces. Thousands will die from rare and strange diseases: AIDS and the Ebola virus being examples. Men will increase in wickedness. Paul puts it this way: "This know also, that in the last days perilous times shall come. For men shall be lovers of their own selves, covetous, boasters, proud, blasphemers, disobedient to parents, unthankful, unholy, without natural affection, trucebreakers, false accusers, incontinent, fierce, despisers of those that are good, traitors, heady, highminded, lovers of pleasures more than lovers of God; having a form of godliness, but denying the power thereof: from such turn away" (2 Timothy 3:1–5).

There is already enough taking place in our world to raise concern, yet it will get worse. John the revelator opens up before our eyes seven dreadful plagues that will afflict the earth. John writes, "And I saw another sign in heaven, great and marvelous, seven angels having the seven last plagues; for in them is filled up the wrath of God" (Revelation 15:1). He continues, "And I heard a great voice out of the temple saying to the seven angels, Go your ways, and pour out the vials of the wrath of God upon the earth. And the first went, and poured out his vial upon the earth; and there fell a noisome and grievous sore upon the men which had the mark of the beast, and upon them which worshipped his image. And the second angel poured out his vial upon the sea; and it became as the blood of a dead man: and every living soul died in the sea. And the third angel poured out his vial upon the rivers and fountains of waters; and they became blood. And I heard the angel of the waters say, Thou art righteous, O Lord, which art, and wast, and shalt be, because thou hast judged thus. For they have shed the blood of saints and prophets, and thou hast given them blood to drink; for they are worthy. And I heard another out of the altar say, Even so, Lord God Almighty, true and righteous are thy judgments. And the fourth angel poured out his vial upon the sun; and power was given unto him to scorch men with fire. And men were scorched with great heat, and blasphemed the name of God, which hath power over these plagues: and they repented not to give him glory. And the fifth angel poured out his vial upon the seat of the beast; and his kingdom was full of darkness; and they gnawed their tongues for pain, And blasphemed the God of heaven because of their pains and their sores, and repented not of their deeds. And the sixth angel poured out his vial upon the great river Euphrates; and the water thereof was dried up, that the way of the kings of the east might be prepared. And I saw three unclean spirits like frogs come out of the mouth of the dragon, and out of the mouth of the beast, and out of the mouth of the false prophet. For they are the spirits of devils, working miracles, which go forth unto the kings of the earth and of the whole world, to gather them to the battle of that great day of God Almighty. Behold, I come as a thief. Blessed is he that watcheth, and keepeth his garments, lest he walk naked, and they see his shame. And he gathered them together into a place called in the Hebrew tongue Armageddon. And the seventh angel poured out his vial into the air; and there came a great voice out of the temple of heaven, from the throne, saying, It is done. And there were voices, and thunders, and lightnings; and there was a great earthquake, such as was not since men were upon the earth, so mighty an earthquake, and so great. And the great city was divided into three parts, and the cities of the nations fell: and great Babylon came in remembrance before God, to give unto her the cup of the wine of the fierceness of his wrath. And every island fled away, and the mountains were not found. And there fell upon men a great hail out of heaven, every stone about the weight of a talent: and men blasphemed

God because of the plague of the hail; for the plague thereof was exceeding great" (Revelation 16:1–21).

Frightening are the coming scenes unveiled by these texts. But when these terrible scourges come upon earth's inhabitants, they will have no affect on the true believers. God *will* deliver His children, in plain sight, for every eye to see. Jesus promised that when the time of trouble comes, He will take care of His people. God declares, "The righteous is delivered out of trouble, and the wicked cometh in his stead. . . . The wicked is snared by the transgression of his lips: but the just shall come out of trouble" (Proverbs 11:8; 12:13).

However, the fact that God will take care of His own does not necessarily mean they will be secretly "raptured." When God sent the plagues down on Egypt, He did not secretly rapture the Israelites out of trouble. Yet while the Egyptians dwelling all around God's people were suffering from vexation, God's children were safe in His care (see Exodus, chapters 5 through 10).

The Lord is able to deliver His people out of trouble as promised. He said, "He that dwelleth in the secret place of the most High shall abide under the shadow of the Almighty. I will say of the LORD, He is my refuge and my fortress: my God; in him will I trust. Surely he shall deliver thee from the snare of the fowler, and from the noisome pestilence. He shall cover thee with his feathers, and under his wings shalt thou trust: his truth shall be thy shield and buckler. Thou shalt not be afraid for the terror by night; nor for the arrow that flieth by day; nor for the pestilence that walketh in darkness; nor for the destruction that wasteth at noonday. A thousand shall fall at thy side, and ten thousand at thy right hand; **but it shall not come nigh thee.** Only with thine eyes shalt thou behold and see the reward of the wicked. Because thou hast made the LORD, which is my refuge, even the most High, thy habitation; **there shall no evil befall thee, neither shall any plague come nigh thy dwelling**" (Psalm 91:1–10).

There are those who are anxious about food and water for that time. In this regard the prophet Isaiah wrote, "Bread shall be given him; his waters shall be sure" (Isaiah 33:16). Psalm 91:11–12 tells us that His angels will keep charge over God's believers to keep them in all their ways. The passage from verse 9 through 16 affirm that He will keep us, protect us, in the time of the plagues.

"The Lord knoweth how to deliver the godly out of temptations, and to reserve the unjust [ungodly] unto the day of judgment to be punished" (2 Peter 2:9). Concerning that time which shall come upon the earth God says, "Come, my people, enter thou into thy chambers, and shut thy doors about [behind] thee: hide thyself as it were for a little moment, until the indignation be overpast. For, behold, the LORD cometh out of his place to punish the inhabitants of the earth for their iniquity: the earth also shall disclose her blood, and shall no more cover her slain" (Isaiah 26:20–21). Yes, God loves His people, and His protection will be clear evidence of His power to save them.

19

A Glorious Second Coming

Many are expecting the long-awaited Messiah to appear somewhere in Jerusalem and restore the Kingdom. According to 1 Thessalonians 4:16–17, Jesus does not touch the earth when He comes. Instead, the waiting saints will meet Him in the sky or, as the verse says, "in the air."

This gathering, or rendezvous, will take place in the air because this is the appointed place specified. Jesus promised that He would come and take us home to heaven. Since He is the One doing the rescuing, He (and not man) has selected the place for the gathering.

The importance of accepting this fact cannot be overemphasized. There is no way Satan can deceive us by counterfeiting Christ's true second coming, for Satan simply cannot accomplish all that Christ has promised will take place:

- Jesus will come in great splendor, glory and power. (See Mark 13:26).
- There will be a "great earthquake." (See Revelation 16:18).
- The heavens will roll back like "a scroll." (See Revelation 6:12–17).
- The wicked will see Him come, and be destroyed. (See Revelation 6:12–17; 2 Thessalonians 2:8).
- The "cities will be broken down," and fall. (See Jeremiah 4:26; Revelation 16:19).
- Every "island [will flee] away," and the "mountains" are moved. (See Revelation 16:20).
- The "righteous" dead will literally and physically rise from their graves. (See 1 Thessalonians 4:14–16).

And, finally, all of God's people—those who have been dead, and those who are alive—will literally meet Him in the air for their long-awaited trip to heaven.

Rapturists predict only a fraction of all that the Bible describes is going to literally transpire at the Second Coming. Because so many important details of the Second Coming are simply left out of rapturist theology, it will not be a great challenge for Satan to produce a false Christ who will walk on the earth and deceive the populace. However, when we accept all that the Bible teaches about the Second Coming, then no one, not even the Devil himself with all of his power and cunning, will be able to reproduce the splendor, glory and power necessary to accomplish all of the earthly and heavenly cataclysmic episodes which will transpire at the Lord's second coming—not to mention the gathering of all of God's children and their transport to heaven.

According to the Bible, we who remain alive unto the coming of the Lord will not be the first to experience translation from earth to heaven. The Scriptures mention two men who have passed through this experience already: Enoch and Elijah.

Concerning Enoch, we read that "by faith Enoch was translated that he should not see death; and was not found, because God had translated him: for before his translation he had this testimony, that he pleased God" (Hebrews 11:5).

Elijah was also taken up into heaven. "And it came to pass, as they still went on, and talked, that, behold, there appeared a chariot of fire, and horses of fire, and parted them both asunder; and Elijah went up by a whirlwind into heaven" (2 Kings 2:11).

These two Biblical examples of human beings defying gravity, death, and corruption, are there for us. They are set as both promises and hope. They are the assurance that eternity is within the reach of all who, like these two men, live godly lives.

Today, astronauts are the only persons fortunate enough to be able to go into space. But the day will soon come when not just a select few, but all who have made the necessary preparations, will be able to take that flight. And what a trip that will be! Speeding through space, we will be able to view many of the splendors and glories our Maker created. Finally, we will arrive at the city. The angels will swing wide the pearly gates and escort us into God's marvelous city. At last we will behold with our own eyes things we could never even have imagined, for "eye hath not seen, nor ear heard, neither have entered into the heart of man, the things which God hath prepared for them that love[d] him" (1 Corinthians 2:9).

20

Tough Times

Tough times just ahead Jesus said, "But pray ye that your flight be not in the winter, neither on the sabbath day" (Matthew 24:20). The question is, Why did He use these illustrations to encourage our preparedness? What do they have in common, and how do they serve to contribute to our readiness?

The urging to pray that the flight be not in the winter had its logic. The admonition has to be taken in the light of the situation. Jesus had already predicted the destruction of Jerusalem. Concerning it, he said, "There shall not be left here one stone upon another, that shall not be thrown down" (Matthew 24:2). "And when ye shall see Jerusalem compassed with armies, then know that the desolation thereof is nigh. Then let them which are in Judea flee to the mountains; and let them which are in the midst of it depart out; and let not them that are in the countries enter thereinto." "Let him which is on the housetop not come down to take any thing out of his house: neither let him which is in the field return back to take his clothes" (Luke 21:20–21; Matthew 24:17–18).

The disciples could see from the warning that when the destruction came, it would be already too late to do anything about it. And since they were to flee to the mountains in a moment's notice without any provisions, that they would perish anyway, if indeed they would have to flee in the winter. Therefore, before it actually took place, they were to pray that it be not in the winter, rather that it would be at some other season. This would provide sufficient time after their escape to prepare for the harsh Palestinian cold. Since winter is generally not considered the appropriate time for preparation, then the illustration forcibly indicates a need for readiness *before* winter.

It was not within their power to dictate the best time for their flight. Clearly, the only One who has the power to alter the events of time is God. Consequently, if their time of flight was to be adjusted, then it would require divine intervention: hence, the admonition to pray. But no one would feel compelled to pray without first believing in the warning. No one would attempt to make a request while having no trust or confidence that the asking would avail anything. Neither would a petitioner make an appeal lacking belief or faith that the One hearing has the ability to do something about the request. So in order to pray, there must exist the *faith* that the solicitor is being heard.

Concerning this, Paul writes, "But without faith it is impossible to please him: for he that cometh to God must believe that he is, and that he is a rewarder of them that diligently seek him" (Hebrews 11:6). It goes without saying that in order to be ready, one must know God. This, however, would never be a reality unless through the process of time one became acquainted with the One who said, "Whatsoever ye shall ask the Father in my name, he will give it you" (John 16:23). So, it is not enough to be a religionist or a churchgoer. We must have saving faith in the One whom at some point in life we have come to know: "who to know is life eternal" (John 17:3–4).

This brings us to the second part of the prayer: "not on the Sabbath day." Just as Noah's flood was a parallel of the end, so was the destruction of Jerusalem. One would expect, therefore, that since the Sabbath was included, along with Jerusalem's predicted destruction, that it will also play an important part in the events associated with the end. Admonishing them to add this to their prayer would then serve to lift the Fourth Commandment to a prominent place in their experience. But why would Jesus refer to the Fourth Commandment as being part and parcel of their readiness? Let us consider several aspects of this Commandment to help us understand.

The Fourth Commandment says: "Remember the sabbath day, to keep it holy. Six days shalt thou labour, and do all thy work: but the seventh day is the sabbath of the LORD thy God: in it thou shalt not do any work, thou, nor thy son, nor thy daughter, thy manservant, nor thy maidservant, nor thy cattle, nor thy stranger that is within thy gates: for in six days the LORD made heaven and earth, the sea, and all that in them is, and rested the seventh day: wherefore the LORD blessed the sabbath day and hallowed it" (Exodus 20:8–11).

This commandment is the only one in the Decalogue that clearly identifies who to worship. A close look at the other nine commandments reveals that they do not positively point out *who* is the recipient of the loyalty or obeisance requested. Only the Sabbath commandment has within it clear identity concerning the One to whom our allegiance should be given.

Like the official United States presidential seal, which has the name, title, and territory or dominion, of the president, the Sabbath carries the same. It declares that He is the Lord—Jehovah is His name. His title is "Creator," and His dominion is "heaven and earth." Who is it then that should receive our love, affections, and our loyalties? There is only One who meets the qualifications mentioned in the Sabbath commandment. Concerning Him, John writes, "In the beginning was the Word, and the Word was with God, and the Word was God. The same was in the beginning with God. All things were made by him; and without him was not any thing made that was made" (John 1:1–3). And in writing to the Colossians, Paul writes, "For by him were all things created, that are in heaven, and that are in earth, visible and invisible, whether they be thrones, or dominions, or principalities, or powers: all things were created by him, and for him: and he is before all things, and by him all things consist" (Colossians 1:16–17). Yes, Jesus Christ is not only *our Creator*, but He is also our *Redeemer*. On the Sabbath He rested from His work of Creation, and on the Sabbath He rested after completing our redemption. To Him belongs our affections, our loyalty, and our love.

The keeping of the Sabbath was also to serve as a weekly sentinel of the spiritual condition. This required day-by-day holy living; for no one can truly keep the Sabbath in its true spirit without having a daily walk with the Lord of the Sabbath. Living out of harmony with His will or living unholy during the week disqualifies one from having communion with a holy God on His appointed day of worship. For He said, "Be ye holy; for I am holy" (1 Peter 1:16).

Since becoming holy is out of man's own ability to accomplish, the transformation from sinner to saint demands Divine intervention. The keeping of the Sabbath then was to serve as a constant reminder of the One who is able to sanctify—or make men holy. He said, "Verily my sabbaths ye shall keep: for it is a sign between me and you throughout your generations; that ye may know that I am the LORD that doth sanctify you" (Exodus 31:13). Yet no one can be holy without being born again. Without this experience, no one can be ready to meet Jesus, for He Himself said, "Except a man be born again, he cannot see the kingdom of God" (John 3:3).

Paul describes this born-again experience by saying, "If any man be in Christ, he is a new creature: old things are passed away, behold, all things are become new" (2 Corinthians 5:17). This denotes a change of heart. One Christian author puts it this way: "Unless he [man] shall receive a new heart, new desires, purposes, and motives, leading to a new life, 'he cannot see the kingdom of God.' " For, "it is impossible for us, of ourselves, to escape from the pit of sin in which we are sunken. Our hearts are evil, and we cannot change them. . . . Education, culture, the exercise of the will, human effort, all have their proper sphere, but here they are powerless. They may produce an outward correctness of behavior, but they cannot change the heart; they cannot purify the springs of life. There must be a power working from within, a new life from above, before men can be changed from sin to holiness. That power is Christ. His grace alone can quicken the lifeless faculties of the soul, and attract it to God, to holiness." Ellen G. White, *Steps To Christ*, p.18.

Jesus, the "Lord also of the sabbath" (Mark 2:28), intended to keep ever before His disciples a daily and weekly reminder of the need they have of Him. Having to pray that their flight would not fall on God's holy day in itself necessitated its observance; otherwise the admonition would be nonsensical. Hence, the forty years of Sabbath observance from its initial prediction down to the destruction of Jerusalem served as a constant daily reminder of their total dependence on the Lord for their daily, weekly, and future security. This prayer, I believe, should not be limited only to the disciples of Jesus' day, but should be made by every believer today as we approach the calamities soon to break upon this earth.

The Sabbath will not only serve as a reminder in this present world, but in fact will serve as a constant emblem of His saving power all through eternity. Isaiah, addressing the now and hereafter, wrote, "If thou turn away thy foot from the sabbath, from doing thy pleasure on my holy day; and call the sabbath a delight, the holy of the LORD, honourable; and shalt honour him, not doing thine own ways: nor finding thine own pleasure, nor speaking thine own words: then shalt thou delight thyself in the LORD; and I will cause thee to ride upon the high places of the earth, and feed thee with the heritage of Jacob thy father: for the mouth of the LORD hath spoken it" (Isaiah 58:13–14).

"For as the new heavens and the new earth, which I will make, shall remain before me, saith the LORD, so shall your seed and your name remain. And it shall come to pass, that from one new moon to another, and from one Sabbath to another, shall all flesh come to worship before me, saith the LORD"(Isaiah 66:22–23). Seeking to return man's secular and materialistic mind back to remember the Creator, John wrote, "And I saw another angel fly in the midst of heaven, having the everlasting gospel to preach unto them that dwell on the earth, and to every nation, and kindred, and tongue, and people, saying with a loud voice, Fear God and give glory to him; for the hour of his judgment is come: and worship him that made heaven, and earth, and the sea, and the fountains of waters. . . . Here is the patience of the saints: here are they that keep the commandments of God, and the faith of Jesus" (Revelation 14:6–7, 12).

Obviously, then, in order to be ready we must be commandment-keeping people. "If thou wilt enter into life," Jesus said, "keep the commandments." When asked which? He said, "Thou shalt do no murder, Thou shalt not commit adultery, Thou shalt not steal, Thou shalt not bear false witness, Honour thy father and thy mother: and Thou shalt love thy neighbour as thyself." And, "if thou wilt be perfect, go sell that thou hast, and give to the poor, and thou shalt have treasure in heaven: and come and follow me" (Matthew 19:17–19, 21). Here Jesus speaks of the Ten Commandments. The first six mentioned refer to man's relation with man, and the second part, "come and follow me," include the first four commandments of the Decalogue; for no one could love and follow Him without obeying all that He asks. To keep one requires that all must be kept. James wrote: "For whosoever shall keep the whole law, and yet offend in one point, he is guilty of all" (James 2:10). Addressing this fact, John wrote, "And hereby we do know that we know him, if we keep his commandments. He that saith, I know him, and keepeth not his commandments, is a liar, and the truth is not in him. But whoso keepeth his word, in him verily is the love of God perfected: hereby know we that we are in him" (1 John 2:3–5).

Keeping the commandments affords us the privilege to enter into the Kingdom, for it is written, "Blessed are they that do his commandments, that they may have right to the tree of life, and may enter in through the gates into the city. For without are dogs, and sorcerers, and whoremongers, and murderers, and idolaters, and whosoever loveth and maketh a lie" (Revelation 22:14–15).

There are those who say that the only duty of a Christian is to love. But love is an ambiguous term. To one person love means sex while to another it may be wrapped up in feelings, emotions, and so forth. The word is subject to being interpreted, depending on a person's background, culture, and experience. The question then remains, What is true love, and on what basis do we judge love?

Others say we should be Christian. But here, too, we enter into utilizing a term that can also be understood in many different ways. Some determine the meaning by the particular church or denomination others belong to. A perfect example is the ongoing religious struggle in Ireland, and also the ethnic cleansing in former Yugoslavia. Another problem with this cliche is that Jesus warned that in the last days there would be false Christs. And, sadly, many have been the victims of following self-proclaimed Christs to their deaths; examples of which are David Koresh in Waco, Texas, and Jim Jones, who led hundreds to end their lives in the early 1980s. Here is another dilemma: Suppose a person did not have the opportunity of knowing what Jesus is really like. Perhaps they have never had the occasion of seeing a genuine Christian example. The question then is, What criteria can be used to aid that person in following the true God? The answer is, The Ten Commandments.

These commandments are a brief transcript of the character of God. God is love! Therefore, a commandment-keeper is not one who uses the law as a checklist by which he can save himself, but rather as a mirror. James says, "But whoso looketh into the perfect law of liberty, and continueth therein, he being not a forgetful hearer, but a doer of the work, this man shall be blessed in his deed" (James 1:25).

In essence the Christian should daily and periodically look into the mirror and see himself. How does he measure up? How much does he really love? "Examine yourselves, whether ye be in the faith; prove your own selves. Know ye not your own selves, how that Jesus Christ is in you, except ye be reprobates" (2 Corinthians 13:5). Correctly understood, the law of the Lord can aid in the process of self-analysis. The commandments then can serve not only as a mirror but also as a means to check the level of my love to God as well as to man. The Psalmist declared, "I delight to do thy will, O my God: yea, thy law is within my heart" (Psalms 40:8). If I truly love, will I rob, steal, or speak evil of my neighbor? No! And, if I truly love God, will I have any god in His place—worship statues or images, take His name in vain (including claiming to be a Christian—Christ-like—and yet demonstrate unchristlike attributes), or disregard His Sabbath? Again, the answer must be unequivocally, No! This is the reason why Paul said, "He that loveth another hath fulfilled the law. For this, Thou shalt not commit adultery, Thou shalt not kill, Thou shalt not steal, Thou shalt not bear false witness, Thou shalt not covet; and if there be any other commandment, it is briefly comprehended in this saying, namely, Thou shalt love thy neighbor as thyself. Love worketh no ill to his neighbour: therefore love is the fulfilling of the law" (Romans 13:8–10).

So as with the disciples, we, too, should seek to be living holy lives, demonstrated by a willing obedience to all of His commandments. We should study His Word daily and seek to apply into our lives what God reveals to us. And we should endeavor by His grace to keep the seventh-day Sabbath, as well as to pray that our flight be not in the winter, nor on the Sabbath day.

21

Escaping the Dreaded Second Death

When our blessed Lord died on Calvary, He did not die to rescue us from death as we know it. The agony that caused His quivering lips to cry out, "My God, my God, why hast thou forsaken me" (Matthew 27:46; Mark 15:34) was not the pangs of physical suffering, but rather the sense of being eternally separated from His Father. This eternal separation is called the "second death."

What Is the Second Death?

Jesus Himself defined the meaning of the second death, when He warned His disciples to "fear not them which kill the body, but are not able to kill the soul: but rather fear him which is able to destroy both soul and body in hell" (Matthew 10:28). In the book of Revelation, Jesus also promised that "He that overcometh shall not be hurt of the second death" (Revelation 2:11).

In contrast to the second death, the first death is of a temporary nature. All of us (up until the second coming of Jesus) will have to experience it. But although it comes to all—the righteous and the wicked, the good and the bad, the rich and the poor—those experiencing the first death can be resurrected. It is not a hopeless vault from which those who enter have no escape.

Jesus was speaking of the first death when He comforted Martha with the words "Thy brother shall rise again." Martha, not realizing what Jesus was really saying, responded, "I know that he shall rise again in the resurrection at the last day." Jesus, in order to make clear what he meant responded, "I am the resurrection, and the life: he that believeth in me, though he were dead, yet shall he live" (John 11:23–25).

To demonstrate that He was the Lifegiver, Jesus then went to the tomb. Though surrounded by skeptics, mourners, and professional wailers, He commanded that the stone blocking the tomb's entrance be rolled away. Then, after offering a word of thanks to His Father, He "cried with a loud voice, Lazarus, come forth! And he that was dead came forth, bound hand and foot with graveclothes: and his face was bound about with a napkin. Jesus saith unto them, Loose him, and let him go" (John 11:43–44).

By this miraculous act of the resurrection of Lazarus, Jesus clarified several things:

#1: He Is the Lifegiver.

In His own words, He said, "I am come that they might have life, and that they might have it more abundantly" (John 10:10).

#2: He Is the Perpetuator of Life.

Jesus not only enhances and enriches the life we now have, but He has power to perpetuate our lives for all eternity. For it is He that "giveth to all life, and breath, and all things" (Acts 17:25). In the words of John, "He that hath the Son hath life; and he that hath not the Son of God hath not life" (1 John 5:12).

In other words, there is no life apart from Jesus, nor is there any hope of entering and continuing eternal life without Him. He is Life, and in order to continue living beyond the tomb, the Lifegiver must be in us.

#3: The First Death Is Not "Final."

In the resurrection of Lazarus, Jesus also showed that the first death is not the final one. Rather, followers of Christ who partake of the first death will also be part of the first resurrection. This is the resurrection that Martha believed in, and of which Jesus also told John the revelator to write: "Blessed and holy is he that hath part in the first resurrection: on such the second death hath no power, but they shall be priests of God and of Christ, and shall reign with him a thousand years" (Revelation 20:6).

This participation in the first resurrection was the experience Paul was referring to when he wrote, "Behold, I shew you a mystery; we shall not all sleep, but we shall all be changed. In a moment, in the twinkling of an eye, at the last trump: for the trumpet shall sound, and the dead shall be raised incorruptible, and we shall be changed. For this corruptible must put on incorruption, and this mortal must put on immortality. So when this corruptible shall have put on incorruption, and this mortal shall have put on immortality, then shall be brought to pass the saying that is written, Death is swallowed up in victory. O death, where is thy sting? O grave, where is thy victory?" (1 Corinthians 15:51–55).

This glorious experience of the first resurrection is what we all want to be a part of—in the event that death should cut short our time on this earth.

Since Jesus speaks assuredly of a "first resurrection," there is safety in assuming that there must also be a second resurrection. And there is, of course. The apostle John alluded to it in Revelation 20:5–6: "But the rest of the dead [writes John] lived not again until the thousand years were finished. This is the first resurrection. Blessed and holy is he that hath part in the first resurrection: on such the second death hath no power, but they shall be priests of God and of Christ, and shall reign with him a thousand years."

So the first resurrection is the resurrection of life: the second, the resurrection of death. These two raisings of the dead were also mentioned by Christ, who admonished His disciples to "Marvel not at this: for the hour is coming, in the which all that are in the graves shall hear his voice, and shall come forth; they that have done good, unto the resurrection of life; and they that have done evil, unto the resurrection of damnation" (John 5:28–29).

The first awakening will usher the participants into life unending—a life that will measure with the life of God. The second will raise all those who will be the recipients of eternal death—the opposite of eternal life.

Words of Assurance

Generally speaking, people are fearful of death, but the Bible gives us these words of assurance through the writings of Paul: "Forasmuch then as the children are partakers of flesh and blood, he also himself likewise took part of the same; that through death he might destroy him that had the power of death, that is, the devil; and deliver them who through fear of death were all their lifetime subject to bondage" (Hebrews 2:14).

Jesus already paid the price! Though He was raised again, He went through the experience of the second, or eternal death, that we might have eternal life.

And so it is not the first death that needs to be dreaded, but the second. While the first death is not final, the second is eternal.

Jesus said, "For God so loved the world, that he gave his only begotten Son, that whosoever believeth in him, should not perish, but have everlasting life" (John 3:16). The word *perish* according to *Strong's Concordance*, means "destroy fully." With Christ there is everlasting life, but without Him the opposite takes place—destruction.

Concerning this destruction, John wrote, "And I saw a great white throne, and him that sat on it, from whose face the earth and the heaven fled away; and there was found no place for them. And I saw the dead stand before God; and the books were opened: and another book was opened, which is the book of life: and the dead were judged out of those things which were written in the books, according to their works. And the sea gave up the dead which were in it; and death and hell delivered up the dead which were in them: and they were judged every man according to their works. And death and hell were cast into the lake of fire. This is the second death. And whosoever was not found written in the book of life was cast into the lake of fire. . . . But the fearful, and unbelieving, and the abominable, and murderers, and whoremongers, and sorcerers, and idolaters, and all liars, shall have their part in the lake which burneth with fire and brimstone: which is the second death" (Revelation 20:11–15; 21:8).

The fire will do its eternal work. The prophet Malachi describes the final result of its work in the following language: "Behold, the day cometh, that shall burn as an oven; and all the proud, yea, and all that do wickedly, shall be stubble: and the day that cometh shall burn them up, saith the LORD of hosts, that it shall leave them neither root nor branch. . . . And ye shall tread down the wicked; for they shall be ashes under the soles of your feet in the day that I shall do this, saith the LORD of hosts" (Malachi 4:1–3).

Escaping the Second Death

Of course, we should all make an effort to escape the second death. The admonition is, "Enter ye in at the strait gate: for wide is the gate, and broad is the way, that leadeth to destruction, and many there be which go in thereat: because strait is the gate, and narrow is the way, which leadeth unto life, and few there be that find it" (Matthew 7:13–14). There is no other way to be ready than to "strive to enter in at the strait gate: for many, I say unto you, will seek to enter in, and shall not be able" (Luke 13:24).

Let us put forth every effort commensurate with our high calling to strive daily through the grace of God to be worthy (if the temporal death should come) of the first resurrection. Paul sums it up like this: "That I may know him, and the power of his resurrection, and the fellowship of his sufferings, being made conformable unto his death; if by any means I might attain unto the resurrection of the dead. Not as though I had already attained, either were already perfect: but I follow after, if that I may apprehend that for which also I am apprehended of Christ Jesus. Brethren, I count not myself to have apprehended: but this one thing I do, forgetting those things which are behind, and reaching forth unto those things which are before, I press toward the mark for the prize of the high calling of God in Christ Jesus" (Philippians 3:10–14).

Our Lord has not left us uninformed concerning the manner of His coming. Jesus made it very clear. He has planned His coming in such a way that no one, not even the devil himself, can counterfeit it. God will not permit Satan to imitate His glorious appearing.

But the Bible does say that the devil will transform himself into an angel of light (see 2 Corinthians 11:14). One writer describes the devil's ploy in the following words: "As the crowning act in the great drama of deception, Satan himself will impersonate Christ. The church has long professed to look to the Saviour's advent as the consummation of her hopes. However, now the great deceiver will make it appear that Christ has come. In different parts of the earth, Satan will manifest himself among men as a majestic being of dazzling brightness, resembling the description of the Son of God given by John in the Revelation, (see Revelation 1:13–15). The glory that surrounds him is unsurpassed by anything that mortal eyes have yet beheld. The shout of triumph rings out upon the air: 'Christ has come! Christ has come!' The people prostrate themselves in adoration before him, while he lifts up his hands and pronounces a blessing upon them, as Christ blessed His disciples when He was upon the earth. His voice is soft and subdued, yet full of melody. In gentle, compassionate tones, He presents some of the same gracious, heavenly truths which the Savior uttered; he heals the diseases of the people . . . the multitudes, from the least to the greatest, give heed to these sorceries, saying; This is the 'great power of God' (Acts 8:10)." *The Great Controversy*, p. 624–625.

Satan will lead the whole world captive in a pleasing infatuation. The people will be led to believe that they are following the Lord—when in reality they will be following the master deceiver. One of the reasons that will contribute to so many falling into this snare is the false description given by many churches of this artful foe. He is usually portrayed as a very evil half-beast-half-human creature. This suits his purpose well, for people then assume that he is capable only of evil. But the greatest error is that which is mixed with truth. Falsehood mixed with truth, holiness mixed with the profane, is what constitutes the greatest deception, and it has always been the most effective way to ensnare people.

When I was a boy, I had a bad habit of going to the refrigerator and helping myself to whatever looked good. I would use my fingers to pick from a bowl, or drink straight from a bottle, making sure all the while that I did not get caught.

One summer day when I was very thirsty, I checked to be sure my mother was not watching, and I went to the refrigerator. I was delighted to find a large Coca-Cola bottle filled to the top. Checking once more to see that no one was around, I grabbed the bottle and put it to my mouth for a refreshing drink. But to my utter disgust, I found myself gulping down bitter black coffee—rather than the sweet taste of Coca-Cola I had expected.

The bottle had the right label and the liquid was the right color, but the taste was quite different! I was fortunate it was just black coffee, for others have not fared nearly so well under similar circumstances. Many have accidentally died from drinking some article bought at the store, thinking they were drinking something good when unbeknown to them, they were taking in poison.

The teaching of the secret rapture, with its attending last-day event scenario, has already served (as in the case of the Australians) to be spiritually delusive. Those who have been tricked by its pleasing subtleties will one day awaken to the reality that they have imbibed a most hellish poison.

Many who teach the secret rapture also believe in a "second chance." They say that after the tribulation and the return of Christ there will be another opportunity for salvation. However, not one of the Bible examples paralleling an "end of time" scenario leaves any room for such an idea. There was no second chance in Noah's or Lot's day. Nothing in the Apocalyptic writings suggests that there will ever be any "second chance." Indeed, the parables of the ten virgins, the wheat and tares, the man without a wedding garment, and people crying "Lord, Lord," all demonstrate that there will be no second chance.

Our Chance Is Now

The truth is, people have an opportunity to accept the Lord every single moment of their lives. If an individual has lived thirty years, then that person has had millions of chances to give himself or herself to God. If an individual has not done so, only God knows what were the circumstances surrounding him that prevented such a commitment. And whatever the reason is—whether it is the love of pleasure, or a job, or money—when a person has heard the invitation and has not decided, it is their choice—which leads us to the sad truth that although people have daily opportunities, most are not taking advantage of them. Consequently, the idea that people will have a second chance after our Lord's return really makes them think that it is not necessary to prepare now.

God wants us to be in a state of readiness at all times. His way, committing ourselves to Christ, is our only safety. So do not assume that there will be any second chance. Do not bank on false promises which can only lead to false security.

I have heard people say, "I'm not going to worry about it. There's a second chance, and I'm going to live my life—really enjoy it and have a ball. Then, when that time comes, I'm going to change." It is hard to imagine people thinking that way, but many do! They venture to put off their preparation until a more convenient season. The devil tempts them with the thought, "You believe in God, and that's what counts now; you can wait."

I am sure that among the antediluvians there were those who also decided to bide their time. Perhaps they presumed upon God's goodness. But whatever they were hoping for, the reality is that once the Flood came, their opportunity was gone. So it will be with Christ's coming. There will remain no future opportunity beyond His appearing—no second chance. Let us not gamble with our destiny. "Wherefore the rather, brethren," Peter urged the believers, "give diligence to make your calling and election sure: for if ye do these things, ye shall never fall: for so an entrance shall be ministered unto you abundantly into the everlasting kingdom of our Lord and Saviour Jesus Christ" (2 Peter 1:10–11).

3ABN
Three Angels Broadcasting
NETWORK
The Miracle Garden
Three Angels Broadcasting Network
P.O. Box 220, West Frankfort, IL 62896 USA
Telephone: (800) 752-3226
Web: www.3abn.org • E-mail: mail@3abn.org